# iPh



*A Detailed Guide to Help you get the Most Out of your iPhone*

*By*

**Albrecht Meyer**

Under no circumstances will any legal responsibility or blame be held against the publisher for any reparation, damages, or monetary loss due to the information herein, either directly or indirectly.

Respective authors own all copyrights not held by the publisher.

The information herein is offered for informational purposes solely, and is universal as so. The presentation of the information is without contract or any type of guarantee assurance.

The trademarks that are used are without any consent, and the publication of the trademark is without permission or backing by the trademark owner. All trademarks and brands within this book are for clarifying purposes only and are the owned by the owners themselves, not affiliated with this document.

# Table of Contents

# Introduction

Apple claims that there is no better place to buy, when it comes to buying a new iPhone, than Apple. The company claims that they have all the answers buyers need for all their questions about carrier service, payment options, and having their new iPhone set up. Apple launched the iPhone 11 on September 10, 2019; it is the latest $699 mobile flagship that offers a range of prominent features at an affordable price tag. Aside from the more costly iPhone 11 Pro and the iPhone 11 Pro Plus, the iPhone 11 is the perfect smartphone for most people. The iPhone 11 replaces the iPhone XR and sports a 6.1-inch LCD display that Apple calls a "Liquid Retina HD Display".

It has a 326ppi resolution of 1792 x 828, a contrast ratio of 1400:1, peak brightness of 625 nits, True Tone support to change the white balance to the ambient light, and extensive color support for real-life colors. Unlike the iPhone XR, the iPhone 11 does not have 3D Touch but does use Haptic Touch instead. Haptic Touch is supported over iOS 13 but lacks 3D touch's pressure response.

Haptic Touch is also supported by the iPhone 11 and 11 Pro, with Apple dropping 3D touch across the iPhone lineup.

Reviews for the iPhone 11 have been mostly positive, with reviewers paying tribute to the new dual-lens camera system with its new ultra-wide-angle lens and Night mode, allowing crisp, transparent images even in low lighting conditions. Reviewers have extolled the iPhone 11's long battery life and low cost. The product is much more affordable than the 11 Pro and Pro Max at $699, and apart from the nature of the display and camera, the 11 is just as right as its more costly counterparts. Reviewers agree that the iPhone 11 is the iPhone that, due to its price tag and feature set, is suitable for most users, but those with an iPhone XS, XS Max, or XR do not want to upgrade because this is an iterative update.

The iPhone 11 is a great phone for anyone with an older iPhone, though. The popular site "Wired" echoed many of these reviews, calling it the iPhone for "just about everyone" and applauding the camera upgrade of the smartphone, stable battery life, low cost, and the A13 Bionic processor's speed.

Apple's UI pattern and outlook for the camera app was highly praised by the forum, pointing out how this enhances the camera as a whole, even though it might not be as good as some on the market.

However, the site pointed to LCD technology of the latest generation, the absence of an in-display fingerprint sensor, and other attributes, but still reported iPhone 11 as a "very good phone" that would have enormous features to sway people to upgrade. The Verge stated its analysis by merely saying, "The iPhone 11 is the phone most people will get this year upgrading to a new iPhone." Engadget addressed the display quality on the iconic iPhone 11, pointing out that its LCD display was the same as in the iPhone XR of the preceding year. Although this is a lower-quality display compared to the OLED, according to the site, "the variations do not matter in day-to-day use". Engadget also liked the iPhone 11's 6.1-inch display size, calling it the sweet spot between the too-small 5.8-inch iPhone 11 Pro and big 6.5-inch iPhone 11 Pro Max. The platform also commended the battery life of the iconic iPhone 11, which averaged nearly 17 hours. As per some reviews, none of the famous sites' positive remarks means that the iPhone 11 is a great phone or that it has all the best apps and specifications you can find. It really is not. So it is perfect where it matters, and anywhere else, it is just wrong. According to them, you can pay $300 more if you want to stay on the cutting edge of tech, and get an iPhone 11 Pro. Yet most people do not have to think it over: just get an iPhone 11. You should be happy!

# Chapter 1: iPhone 11- A Long Journey

At the Macworld 2007 conference in San Francisco, former Apple CEO Steve Jobs unveiled the iPhone to the public on January 9, 2007. That same year, on June 29, it went on sale. Apple marketed 13 million iPhones in the first five quarters of the product available on the market. Since its debut, the number of iPhones sold in 2010 has surpassed 70 million. Apple announced that 100 million iPhones had been sold in 2011. The same year, Apple eclipsed Nokia with the most annual sales as a cell phone maker. Apple launches new iPhone models on a frequent basis, adding new features and improvements in design. As of 2017, iPhone X (pronounced iPhone 10) was the latest iteration, removing the standard Home button in favor of a full touchscreen interface. Had it not been for the latest equipped, fast-paced technology, the high tech generation would never have witnessed such a commendable launch by Apple.

## 1.1 Technology and Smart Phones

Smartphones have revolutionized our lives over the past decade in ways that go far beyond how we communicate. In addition to calling, texting and emailing, more than two billion people around the world are now using these devices to navigate, book cab rides, compare product reviews and prices, follow the news, see movies, listen to the music, play video games, memorize holidays and, last but not least, participate in social media.

The equipment used in wireless communication is mobile technology. In the recent few years, mobile technology has developed rapidly. A typical portable computer has gone from being just a two-way pager to being a cell phone, a GPS navigation system, an integrated web browser and an instant messaging application, and a portable gaming console since the start of this millennium. Many experts think the future of computer technology rests with wireless networking in mobile computing. Mobile computing is becoming more popular by way of tablet computers. Tablets can be used with the help of the 3G and 4G networks. In different fields, mobile technology has various definitions, primarily mobile technology in information technology and mobile technology in basketball technology.

## The Convergence of Mobile Communications

In 1890 Tesla laid the theoretical groundwork for wireless communication. In 1894 Marconi, regarded as the father of radio, transmitted electrical signals for the first time two miles away. Mobile technology has brought tremendous change to human society. You may also trace the use of mobile devices in government departments back during the World War I era. The convergence of mobile communications technology and information technology has made mobile technology the focal point of industry focus in recent years.

Mobile technology has slowly evolved with the convergence of mobile communication and mobile computing technologies. The mobile connectivity brought about by the implementation and growth of mobile technologies has provided online links and contact for Ubiquitous Computing and anytime, anywhere in the Liaison. The sharing of knowledge provides incentives, introduces new opportunities and challenges to mobile work, and facilitates more improvements in social and organizational types.

## The Mobile Communications Sector

**0G:** An early cell phone system developed in the 1970s.

Though mobile briefcase-type phones have emerged at this time, they usually still need to be mounted in a car or truck.

**0.5G:** It is the technology band, which improves the essential technical characteristics of 0G.

**1G:** Refers to the first generation of wireless telecommunications technology, namely fixed cellular mobile phones. The analog cellular, portable radiotelephone standards were adopted in the 1980s.

**2G:** Second-generation Wireless Phone. 2G networks are primarily for voice communications only, except that some specifications can also use SMS messages as a means of data transmission.

**2.5G:** It is a selection of cellular technologies evolving between 2G and 3G. This includes digital communication tools that support email and smooth web browsing in addition to voice.

**2.75G:** means the technology that, while not meeting 3G specifications, plays a 3G role in the industry.

**3 G:** Representing the third generation of digital networking technology, it incorporates cellular broadband audio, data, and multimedia communications technologies.

**3.75G:** It is the technology that goes beyond robust 3G wireless and mobile technology growth.

**4G:** Named for high-speed mobile wireless networking technology and planned to enable new data networks and immersive mobile television services.

**5G:** Enhances 4G, provides faster response times (lower latency), and higher data transmission rates.

In the mid-1980s, 1G was presented as voice-just correspondence by means of "brick phones". Later in 1991, the improvement of 2G presented Short Message Service (SMS) and Multimedia Messaging Service (MMS) capacities, permitting picture messages to be sent and gotten between phones. In 1998, 3G was launched to give quicker information transmission rates to help with video calling and internet access. 4G was discharged in 2008 to help all the more requesting administrations, for example, gaming administrations, HD portable TV, video conferencing, and 3D TV. 5G innovation has got ready for the forthcoming future.

**4G networking**

4G is the current standard cell service offered to mobile phone clients, and its execution is multiple times quicker than 3G administration.

One of the essential spotlights in the 4G versatile systems is the control of rapid bundle transmissions or burst traffic in the channels. Similar codes utilized in the 2G-3G systems are applied to 4G versatile or remote networks. The identification of short blasts will be a significant issue because of their helpless fractional relationship properties.

An ongoing report has demonstrated that customary multilayer arrange engineering dependent on the Open Systems Interconnection (OSI) model may not be feasible for a 4G versatile system, where exchanges of small parcels will be the signature piece of the traffic in the channels. As the parcels from various mobiles convey totally extraordinary channel attributes, the beneficiary ought to execute every single fundamental calculation, for example, channel estimation, collaborations with every single upper layer, etc., inside a 'brief' timeframe.

### 5G networking

5G's presentation objectives are high information rates, decreased inertness, vitality reserve funds, diminished costs, expanded framework limit, and huge scope gadget network.

The preferred fundamental position of 5G systems is that the information transmission rate is a lot higher than the past cell organize, up to 10Gbit/s, which is quicker than the current wired Internet and multiple times quicker than the past 4G LTE cell arrange. Another benefit is lower organized idleness (speedier reaction time), under one millisecond, and 4G is 30-70 milliseconds.

The pinnacle rate needs to arrive at the Gbit/s standard to meet the high information volume of top-notch video, and computer-generated reality, etc. The air interface postpones level should be around 1ms, which meets ongoing applications, for example, independent driving and telemedicine.

- It has a vast system limit, giving the association limit of 100 billion gadgets to meet IoT correspondence.
- The range effectiveness is multiple times higher than LTE.
- With constant extensive zone inclusion and high portability, the client experience rate arrives at 100 Mbit/s.
- The stream thickness and the number of associations are extraordinarily expanded.

- The framework is synergistic, and the degree of knowledge is improved. It is portrayed by multi-client, multi-point, multi-radio wire, multi-admission synergistic systems administration, and adaptable programmed modification between systems.

### Fate of 5G

### Quicker Web Speed

Quicker system pace ought to be everybody's most profound comprehension of 5G. For an increasingly natural model, downloading a top-notch film with 5G would not take over one second.

### Telephone Update Emphasis

The cell phones utilized today may become "old collectibles" later on. As a result of the coming of 5G, there are sure prerequisites for hardware. In the event that cell phone needs to utilize 5G organize, the processor needs to help 5G baseband and bolster ultra-high recurrence band. The most elevated rate and transfer speed must satisfy the guideline.

### Broad Utilization of Cloud Innovation

Most definitely, it might at present be utilized to watch motion pictures, talk and mess around on the Internet; however, 5G is, to a higher degree, an information issue.

Fast speed is significant for cloud innovation. Later on, the information will be transferred to the cloud, and work, life, and amusement will be conveyed to the cloud.

## 1.2 Benefits of Smart Phones

After just about ten years, cell phone evolution is fruitful to such an extent that organizations and employees face complications envisioning a day not having them. Besides making calls, almost all the cell phones today could locally provide directions through GPS, take pictures, play the music, and monitor arrangements and contacts. Through the establishment of applications, the purpose of smartphones increases significantly and develops continually.

Businesses can utilize this quickly, developing innovation. To a specialist, a cell phone gives the capacity to arrange and agree with accomplices whenever and wherever required. It is difficult to envision how less profitable an entrepreneur would be in the event when he was unable to finish up an agreement, make arrangements, or unravel some other issues while being outside the workplace. Then again, smartphones have spared life multiple times. An individual who wound up in a dangerous circumstance can call for help by utilizing a smartphone.

Makers incorporate plenty of extra highlights into present-day cell phones. For instance, a GPS module's accessibility is presently a common thing for a brilliant device of each brand and maker. This is not even the primary element of the phone. However, numerous individuals utilize such applications as Google Maps, which assists with exploring in an outside city.

Additionally, there are such vast numbers of elective methods of utilizing a cell phone. Your device might be used as a TV controller, remote game controller, webcam, standardized tag scanner, e-wallet, or electronic pass. It appears that the rundown is perpetual—these alternatives further and additionally coordinate cell phones into the tech space around the individual.

In this sub-section, we plan to teach individuals about the unlimited prospects and critical advantages of cell phones in our lives. We need to publicize the benefits of a smart cell phone and show that this incredible creation is not just for a young age. The more established individuals can likewise make a ton of parts of their life a lot simpler with the assistance of a cell phone. We live in a period of versatile innovation and simply should have the option to utilize the entirety of its favorable circumstances to make our life increasingly agreeable.

Below are some of the amazing merits of smartphones:

**1. Contrasting Communication Options**

Old school phones can call and text. While this could convey the desired information; cell phones permit you various methods of interacting with your employees, clients, and related contacts. Not just would they be able to call, text, and IM, these specialized instruments give you access to email, quick photograph sharing, video calling, and video conferencing. You can seat a workforce gathering from anyplace you have smartphone accessibility! You can likewise stay associated through person to person communication locales like Twitter, Facebook, and LinkedIn.

**2. Investigating the Web**

How regularly every day do you counsel the web for news or other data fundamental to your business? Initially, web perusing took place at a workplace in an office, where a wire could approach the PC. Far away access and PCs moved the web to essentially anyplace inside the home or office. Yet, cell phone upgrade, with the inclusion of broadband remote, has directed the web onto the metro, into the vehicles, and to the recreation center.

Likewise, the most recent cell phones can show about as a significant part of the web as PCs, including business news locales and spilling top-notch recordings.

### 3. From Many Devices to One

Once, you may have needed a whole pack to haul around all the gadgets required for everyday business exercises. You would expect your pager, mobile phone, and your PDA. Likewise, you may require an MP3 player, a digital book peruser, a camera, and a GPS gadget. Through scaled-down device that packs a processor, speakers, a camera, a GPS recipient, a Wi-Fi connector and a top-quality touch-delicate screen into a mobile phone estimated gadget, a smartphone places the entirety of such usefulness inside your pocket. One of your laborers could without much of a stretch quest for bearings to a customer's business, read a business flier before a gathering begins, and transmit a promotion deal to your office by means of a portable hotspot.

### 4. Accessibility of Many Applications

The late-twentieth-century had seen an immense arrival of PC application. The mid-twenty-first century also brings about a vast number of cell phone applications.

The sensors incorporated within the smartphone have made it a gadget with literally limitless applications. Besides the ample amounts of games (your workers would require frequent breaks), there are different effectiveness applications approachable to spare a smart thought when motivation strikes, compose meeting notes, and render multiple prospects. Along with your staff, you can stay in shape with well-being and wellness applications to follow miles strolled and the calories you have devoured. Web radio and podcasting applications put you in contact with totally different universes of sound. Compass applications, leveling applications, and electric lamps give handheld utilities. Applications that let you paint change photographs or make music tap into your inventiveness.

In the hustles of present-day life, there are such a great number of significant components. You may end up with an occupied and frenzied calendar. There are specific components of your life that you should sift through and sort out. It is essential to have a timetable and to design things to make your life run smoother.

Therefore, one of the most important gadgets you can use to help with your life is smartphones. By any option, if you do possess a smartphone, you might realize how significant they are.

There is a lot that you could practice with a cell phone; thus, there is a wide range of manners by which they perform a crucial job in your life. On the off chance that you do not yet have a cell phone, you have to consider getting one at that point.

## 1.3 Apple's Journey to iPhone 11

On 2 August, 2018, the Apple impacted the world forever by turning into the world's initial $1 trillion organization, estimated by advertise capitalization. Though it did see some downfall in the later half during the year, enduring a deficit above $450 billion during the final quarter in 2018, it has managed to retain the more significant part of that sum ever since, and now remains at around $967.87 billion since September 2019. Since 2010, (AAPL) i.e.

Apple has turned up among the most influential organizations on the planet. It has involved the top space on a yearly premise since 2012 onwards, having certain intermittent maneuvering for position among it and (XOM) Exxon.

The explanation Apple is esteemed so exceptionally is straightforward on a superficial level: the organization makes mainstream items with liberal edges.

Notwithstanding, if the inquisitive peruser burrows somewhat more profound, it will discover botches, ousted CEOs, and significantly more. This particular section, will take a glimpse at long journey behind Apple's prosperity.

### Apple and the Steve Jobs

Before comprehending why Apple has such an impact today, it would first be valuable to investigate its starting points and history. Beginning from the primary Apple PC (Apple I, was only a motherboard with no screen or console) to the most recent iWatch, let us have a short review of the order of Apple's inventive items:

Macintosh, established by Steve Wozniak and Steve Jobs, began in the matter of unit PCs with Apple I. Such underlying creation runs, albeit mainstream as collectible presently, was chiefly associated with helping the organization get enough cash-flow to manufacture Apple II during 1977 - that year, Apple authoritatively joined. Wozniak principally assembled both these PCs, and Jobs took care of the showcasing part.

Apple II brought in the organization's income until mid-1980s, in spite of the equipment remaining, to a great extent, the equivalent.

Apple endeavored refreshes such as Apple III as well as Apple Lisa.

However, these neglected to get on monetarily. In spite of the fact that Apple II had been all the while selling, Apple itself as an organization was in a difficult situation towards the start of 80s.

The 1984 arrival of Macintosh had been a jump ahead for Apple, however in the interceding a very long time between the Macintosh and Apple II, IBM had made up for the last time. Macintosh's disillusioning incomes and inward battles for control prompted Apple's board excusing Jobs for John Sculley. Steve moved away from Apple to chip away at NeXT Inc. Fortunately under the Sculley, Apple began developing its product offerings.

Sculley filled in as Apple's CEO up until 1993. In those years, the organization (Apple) appreciated solid development as it made new items, including the Macintosh Portable, laser printers, the PowerBooks, Newton, and substantially more. Apple items kept on selling, including some hidden costs, so the edges were liberal for Apple while prompting solid monetary outcomes. During a similar period, in any case, modest PCs running Windows served a whole lot bigger center market for individuals who needed home PCs; however, they could not manage the cost of a Mac. Examination revealed that Apple appeared to slow down, although it was bringing in cash.

Two CEOs, Gil Amelio and Michael Spindler bombed attempting to switch things around on the persistent IBM clones extension running Microsoft. The working framework, Windows, of Microsoft's was turning into the business standard, and Apple's OS was giving indications old enough. Amelio tended to the OS problems by purchasing NeXT Inc. - an organization governed by previous Apple author Steve Jobs.

**The Second Opportunity CEO**

From the Macintosh presentation ahead, Apple has been either an impression of or response to the Steve Jobs' administration. In Macintosh, Apple attempted to make a gadget that made processing straightforward and agreeable for the client. Specifically, Jobs was about to make a client experience that might persuade everybody to purchase a Mac. He believed that a progressive item could not rely upon clients' needs because the client cannot comprehend the nature of the item until the individual is occupying it. Lamentably, he was relatively revolutionary in 1985 - accurately 12 years comparatively ahead of time.

When Jobs ousted Amelio and retook the reigns of Apple in 1997, the hardware had made up for the lost time to his vision for everything computerized.

He propelled the iMac with a robust advertising effort, highlighting the "Think Different" motto. Even though Jobs is regularly given acknowledgment for investing the cash and energy in showcasing, Apple has consistently been fantastic at advertising and marking. The genuine distinction between the iMac and all the items going before it was the magnificence. Its screen arrangement was not like any other PC available in the market. The iMac nearly seemed like a racer's head protector shot at speed, a bright haze clearing once more from the screen. In 1998, the iMac was the most stylishly satisfying gadget available. It was the PC nobody realized they needed until they saw it. It was rich and, gratitude to the OS update, it was easy to understand.

**The iCommunity**

The iMac was only the beginning as Apple discharged a string of hit items that mirrored the new spotlight on style and client experience. These incorporated the iBook, the iPod, the iPhone, the MacBook Air, and the iPad. The iPod turned into the classification executioner in MP3 players; the iPhone propelled and afterward overwhelmed the cell phone advertise. Some way or another, the iPad persuaded millions regarding individuals that they required one more screen to expend content on.

These gadgets were seen as being better in quality - and surely in the plan - than contending items. Jobs was determined on the plan and taught the whole culture of Apple into the craft of structure. The other point he took Apple back to in his subsequent residency is the usability. Following a couple of moments of utilizing the wheel on an iPod or tapping symbols on an iPad, these new types of control turned out to be a piece of the effortlessness that makes Apple so engaging. Presently every item update from Apple is foreseen by the media and the overall population notwithstanding the fans that the organization had from the beginning.

All the more critically, these items moved Apple into another plan of action of making a healthy ecosystem of content, software, and hardware. Macintosh did not make iTunes, a straightforward program for clients to move MP3s onto iPods, just like the case with many other makers' contributions. Instead, the organization assaulted the idea of a collection by breaking them into melodies that would be sold exclusively at a small portion of the entire collection cost. A similar procedure occurred with programming. Numerous famous PC capacities should be possible on Apple's cell phones utilizing stripped-down applications - accessible obviously, on Apple's App Store.

As the vast primary mover into a significant number of these business sectors, Apple assembled the arena and set the game's standards. When you pay for books, motion pictures, applications, or music on an Apple gadget, Apple gets a cut. This business does not produce as much income as selling an iPhone or an iPad, where the markup is significantly more liberal.

It is the content you purchase through Apple that secures numerous individuals in purchasing Apple again when their I-gadget jumps on in years. Hence, the ecosystem's content element pays off for Apple for the time being and the long haul. When you relocate to Apple, given the structure or the effortlessness, it is the mix with your content that keeps you there.

**The Post-Jobs Period**

Steve Jobs passed away in 2011 due to pancreatic cancer. Filling in as CEO until in no time before his passing, Steve Jobs surrendered the reins of the organization to Tim Cook. The post-Jobs period at Apple has, in any case, been a triumph by most measures, with Apple proceeding to be the predominant tech organization in both pieces of the overall industry and stock cost.

In any case, a few examiners feel that without Jobs as the inventive power, Apple has gotten exclusively iterative in its tech discharges instead of transformative. The significant arrival of the post-Jobs time has been the Apple Watch. Without the launch of an innovative new item, Apple is intensely dependent on the creation pattern of the iPhone to control its money related achievement. Critics state that without Steve Jobs in charge, Apple has lately lost its inventive edge and is riding on its image to drive deals. Its Apple Watch, for example, had not drawn similar energy and clique following as its iPhone did when it was first propelled.

On September 10, 2019, Apple held an online networking occasion where it declared new services and upgraded releases of related items. In numerous regards, the 2019 declaration was almost the same. Apple revealed another membership service for computer games called Apple Arcade. A report in regards to its Apple TV+ spilling video-on-request service was first declared in March of 2019. However, other forthcoming contributions are mainly centered on the upgrades to the existing items.

The seventh era iPad, for example, incorporates an extended 10.2-inch Retina screen just as some additional performing multiple task highlights; however, it is anything but a discount modification of the well-known tablet.

The fifth era Apple Watch incorporates an upgraded display. However, the item that speculators and clients are generally quick to find out about, in any case, is the most recent versions of the iPhone, Apple's notorious cell phones.

Numerous years prior in a chilly winter morning in January, in 2007, to be exact, the absolute first iPhone was divulged at the Macworld occasion in San Francisco. Macworld used to be a serious deal in those days, and the Apple fellow benefactor and afterward CEO, the Late Steve Jobs acquainted the first-ever iPhone with the world. Around then, it was contributed as three items: one—a widescreen iPod with a touchscreen, a cell phone to heft around and be associated, and a web gadget for perusing the profundities of the Internet.

The iPhone was put up for sale after that.

The iPhone, over the previous decade, has been the benchmark phone at different occurrences. It practically re-imagined what a cell phone implied, as far as the software and the hardware were concerned. Not, at this point, were resistive touchscreens, terrible structures, low-quality showcases, and lazy execution going to be endured by buyers, who were seeing the new meanings of client experience.

The initial ten years of the excursion were most likely a little smoother, yet the only thing steady is the change—Android lead rivals have been coordinating (and in any event, enhancing) certain viewpoints, off late. Be it the mix of ground-breaking hardware, an altogether improved Android programming, and a more prominent spotlight on advancement, past merely the spec sheet, the opposition from the Android ecosystem is presently more worthy of being noted than any time in recent memory the Apple iPhone to battle with.

While it is difficult to pack just about ten years' worth of features, here is a portion of the champion minutes in the iPhone's excursion. The time is given below.

**2007 Era: iPhone**

It was the absolute first iPhone and was, in fact, progressive and revolutionary at that time. Touchscreen cells were new and special for buyers then—the very iPhone contained a 3.5-inch display that was multi-touch. The structure was unique and different from the cell phones which existed in the market previously. Shoppers enjoyed what they saw; obviously—approximately 6.1 million of the iPhones were marketed that year itself.

One needs to feel a little for Nokia, which is although presently on a rebound trail, yet supposedly dumped a touchscreen idea two or three years earlier. Perhaps things would have had been altogether different for Nokia.

### 2008 Era: iPhone 3G

Similarly, as its name proposed, the enormous expansion in this version was that of 3G versatile system capacity—truly, 3G was a serious deal in those days. Different augmentations included GPS capacities for area following and route. In any case, what this iPhone is affectionately associated with is; it was initial iPhone that had the App Store, plus the capacity to download as well as run outsider applications. This iPhone likewise included push-email. The urge for iPhone was very high when the 3G version of iPhone was propelled, and around 1 million cells were marketed during the main seven day stretch of dispatch. At this point, telephone producers, such as Nokia and BlackBerry (and even Microsoft partly), were attempting to comprehend what had smacked them in the face. The weak reactions from the customers, maybe best displayed by the poor quality Nokia 5800 XpressMusic phone, just demonstrated how a long way behind Apple's competitors were.

### 2009 Era: iPhone 3GS

It was the very first occasion when Apple truly concentrated on autonomy and control. "The quickest, most remarkable iPhone so far," was how iPhone 3GS got marketed. This pressed in an all the more impressive processor and contained more RAM plus the extra space than the earlier iPhone 3G. That event was maybe the beginning stage for all the hardware fights that cell phone producers have enjoyed throughout the years. iPhone 3GS additionally offered near 1 million during the primary seven day stretch of dispatch. With iOS 3, Apple, at last, presented a few highlights that were prominently absent from iPhones up until now, including the capacity to cut and reorder text.

### 2010 Era: iPhone 4

This fourth-generation iPhone witnessed a new structure language, containing a hardened steel outline, level sides, and also the glass on front part and back portion. This was additionally the initial iPhone that helped the CDMA versatile systems in different nations. Execution stayed in the center—this currently had significantly extra RAM (about 512MB compared to iPhone 3GS, that contained 256MB RAM) so as to permit better application execution since outsider applications were a fury. iPhone 4 highlighted the principal Retina show in cell phones.

### 2011 Era: iPhone 4S

Great deal changed in the 4S version of iPhone, however, outwardly it appeared to be indistinguishable from iPhone 4. The said touchphone was reported a day prior to Steve Jobs' demise. It stuffed in a refreshed processor just as a superior camera. Alongside the advanced iOS 5 working framework, the 4S version of iPhone acquainted the world with a voice acknowledgment tool, i.e., Siri, along with the storage administration, i.e., iCloud were extraordinary recommendations at that point.

### 2012 Era: iPhone 5

This iPhone version introduced a great deal of stuff that stays a piece of the most recent lineup of the Apple iPhones, too—Lightning connector used for the charging and information move (the iPhones had utilized a more extensive 30-pin connector up till now) along with the earbuds. The structure invigorates likewise incorporated a screen dimension increment from the 3.5 creeps to about 4 inches, also a more slender aluminum framework. Backing for LTE portable systems was likewise presented. Around 5 million plus phones were marketed during the initial three days when the iPhone 5 hit the racks.

### 2013 Era: iPhone 5S, plus the iPhone 5C

For the very first moment Apple launched two diverse iPhones around the same time, with similar screen sizes. The 5S version of iPhone was an intelligent replacement for iPhone 5. It held a similar structure and just the same measurements. However, inside the mechanism was another 64-piece processor (seen without precedent for a cell phone), an enhanced camera, a Touch ID unique mark scanner coordinated into home catch, and also the M7 "movement. The "co-processor," permitted fitness tracking too. The 5C version was taken as a progressively moderate iPhone having a polycarbonate external covering and different shading alternatives; however, it did not set sale outlines ablaze.

### 2014 Era: iPhone 6 and the iPhone 6 Plus

It was Apple's first experience presenting two iPhones having differing screen sizes. The iPhone 6 had got a 4.7-inch front screen while the 6S iPhone had a 5.5-inch screen. Plan was essentially invigorated too, and the latest iPhones were more slender as well. It was the first instance when 128GB capacity alternatives were too on offer. There was, be that as it may, the whole "Bendgate" furor after certain clients revealed that 6 Plus was twisting when exposed to pressure under specific circumstances.

**2015 Era: iPhone 6S, 6S Plus**

Adhering to the pattern of "s" lineup throughout the years, 6S and 6S Plus had been all the more remarkable upgrades of 6 and the 6 Plus versions. The structure continued as before, just as the size of the screen. A more current processor and enhanced camera were different features. Apple changed to a more grounded 7000 arrangement aluminum combination case, to respond to the complaints of 6000 arrangement aluminum bowing in the previous versions. It was then that Rose Gold shading choice was made accessible—a shading that has since been embraced by practically so many phone producers. These iPhones additionally presented the 3D contact innovation, which identifies the contrasting weight of your finger's touch on iPhone's screen and permits faster access to application menus and executes certain jobs faster. The hardware for the Touch ID was also improved, which diminished the unique mark filter time.

**2016 Era: iPhone SE**

iPhone SE release, to be completely forthright, was somewhat unforeseen. Apple genuinely accepted that customers needed a littler screen size. Therefore the arrival of 4-inch show previously observed on iPhone 5 and the 5s preceding this.

The structure was additionally similar to that of iPhone 5, to such an extent that a considerable lot of the prior adornments, for example, the cases, went well with iPhone SE as well. The internals was first class, however, and precisely reproduced iPhone 6s, which was most recent hardware mix.

### 2016 Era: iPhone 7 and 7 Plus

So much changed with seven iPhone versions. The 3.5mm earphone jack had last been granted the send-off in the two phones, and water aversion was included. Both the displays were 25% more extravagant and can imitate a larger number of hues than the forerunner. The 7 Plus gets the double camera and the optical zoom as well. The Jet dark (lustrous) and dark (matte) shading alternatives were generally welcomed. Regarding execution, these had been the most remarkable iPhones to date.

### 2017 Era: iPhone 8 and 8 Plus Releases

Apple truly placed up the great deal with this launch. 8 and 8 Plus versions of iPhone executed the incredible A11 Bionic operator. Regarding the display, these looked fundamentally the same as the ancestors, aside from one important modification—the glass sheet at the back that empowered remote charging, while making these initial iPhones to render that.

The cameras had been improved en route, while the True-Tone show included was currently a standard choice.

**2017 Era: iPhone X**

This was the enormous one. It turned out to be the greatest iPhone advancement in years. The home catch which had lived underneath the showcase throughout recent years, had now gone. The screen got taller, this turned into the initial iPhone having an OLED display. There was an upper indent which isolated remarks as fast as it partitioned the notice bar on interface of iOS 11. Face ID picture acknowledgment innovation supplanted the unique mark sensor, and the double cameras at the back had been prepared for AR applications. This possessed a more significant presentation than the 8 Plus iPhone (5.8-inch compared to 5.5-inch) still was progressively minimal to grasp and impressively lighter. This was the point at which the difficulties had gotten more grounded for iPhones from Apple and incredible Android lead phones coming in our direction.

**2018 Era: iPhone XS and XS Max**

This expected development truly knocked up the stakes on the preparing front.

The latest iPhones, operating A12 Bionic unit was as much as is 15 percent quicker than the astounding A11 Bionic.

The Bionic chip of A11 could perform 600 billion calculations for each second. In contrast, the contemporary A12 Bionic could proceed upwards of 5 trillion calculation activities for each second, which additionally benefited the facial identification feature of the Face ID. The 6.5-inch show of XS Max version of iPhone is the biggest ever in iPhone. Apple likewise included the double SIM usefulness, after numerous long periods of clients requesting it. Yet, in another symbol—one of SIM spaces here would be a simulated SIM, otherwise called e-SIM. By and by, these versions of iPhones were fundamentally increasingly costly as well. The opposition is at its pinnacle. On the minus side, we are to discuss the experience, camera execution, and generally speaking client experience. The current iPhones face noteworthy rivalry from any semblance of the Samsung Galaxy S9+, the Google Pixel 3 territory, the OnePlus six, and OnePlus 6T just as the Huawei Mate 20 Pro.

**2018 Era: iPhone XR**

Various reviewers said that XR might be the reasonable iPhone that everyone had been longing for. Many others said this would be the arrival of iPhone 5c. It did not turn out to be one or the other.

It was unmistakably delightful, accessible in numerous hues. In many regards, it was as competent and ground-breaking as iPhone XS as well as XS Max, besides the single back-camera. It still confined the Portrait photography mode. The said version had an LCD show rather than an OLED—it is labelled as the Liquid Retina by the Apple. Also, for most expectations and purposes, XR carries out the responsibility done. The cost stays a factor, however.

**2019 Era: iPhone 11, 11 Pro, Pro Max Versions**

Let us look at the variations between these three components of the 11 series in the upcoming section of this chapter.

## 1.4 Difference between iPhone 11 Series

**iPhone 11:** This iPhone release has been displayed as the most reasonable of Apple's yearly rollout; however, it, despite everything, had enough advantages to be one of the year's most well-known models. It flaunts; its 6.1-inch Liquid Retina shows with six varieties of eye-getting hues. The most significant hit comes as the second camera on the rear of the model. You are not losing any quality either, as the two cameras have 12 MP and numerous broad and ultra-wide focal points available to you.

**Pro version of iPhone 11:** Some devoted Apple clients are not enthusiasts of the bigger screens. In the event like that, 11 Pro iPhone version would be a much-needed refresher. The Super Retina XDR show that is 5.5-inch is a progressive, apparent contribution to deal with all your photography needs. In the crazy update, there is a highlighting of three focal points of 12 MP HDR camera, easily gifting the client with wide, the ultra-wide, along with the zooming focal points. The shading alternatives are not as striking as the customary iPhone 11. However, there are many respectable smartphone cases out there standing by to tidy up the outside.

**Pro Max version of the iPhone 11:** The biggest - and priciest - model of 2019 would be the iPhone 11 Pro Max. Its XDR Display for the Super Retina is shocking, gelling with its adequate 6.5" size. Likewise, it incorporates a similar three-focal point camera arrangement in the 11 Pro version, giving a passage into a striking new universe of photography. You can expect the same shading plans between the two models. However, the principle contrast is the screen's size, which may be the kicker for some fanatic Apple fans.

# Chapter 2: Guide to iOS 13

The present operating system for Apple's iPhone 11 is iOS 13. This operating system has been, likewise, Apple's most up to date working framework for iPhones and iPads up until this point. Its highlights incorporate a Dark Mode, a Find My application, a redid Photos application, a new Siri voice, refreshed protection highlights, new road level view for Maps, and so much more. The current adaptation of iOS 13 is iOS 13.6, discharged to general society on July 15. iOS 13.6 presents a switch for tweaking upgrades, offering iOS clients to empower an alternative that forestalls iPhones and iPads from downloading new iOS upgrades when associated with Wi-Fi.

iPhone demands the most recent verified programming system. Introducing other programming renditions (e.g., Beta adaptations, unapproved programming variants, and so on.) could cause issues with actuation, applications, and other gadget usefulness.

- iOS updates can be either discretionary or programmed.
- The on-screen prompts of the iOS download, reinforcement, and update may fluctuate.

- Before going for an update, back up your iPhone.
- If the gadget neglects to reboot after the iOS update, restart the device.
- The iOS update procedure may take a few minutes; do not intrude while in progress.
- To keep away from potential information charges, it is prescribed to interface with a Wi-Fi arrangement.
- The Cellular Data update technique may not be accessible for all iOS refreshes.

**iOS Upgrade through the Cellular system or Wi-Fi**

**Note:** Do ensure Wi-Fi is turned on if you are performing update utilizing Wi-Fi.

- Press the Power button if the gadget does not turn on consequently.
- Whenever incited, slide the Unlock switch right, to open the device.
- From the Home screen, explore Settings Icon > General > Software Update.
- Tap Download and Install.

**Note:** If incited, enter your password.

- Go through the Terms and Conditions and, at that point, tap Agree.

- When the product update is finished, swipe up from the base of the screen to turn on the gadget.

**iOS Update utilizing your Mac or the PC**

- From the PC, shut any apps that were open.
- Press Power option to turn the iPhone on.
- Do one of the accompanying:

**Note:** For help checking your macOS variant, consult the Apple assistance page.

- On the off chance that utilizing a Mac through the macOS Catalina 10.15, select Finder.
- On the off chance that using a Mac through the macOS Mojave 10.14 or prior or a PC, select the iTunes.
- Associate your gadget to your PC utilizing the USB link provided then find the device.
- Note: For help with finding the gadget, allude to the Apple assistance page.
- Snap' General' or 'Settings' at that point, click Check for Update.

- Snap Download and Update.
- Whenever incited, enter your password.

**Update iOS by itself**

**Note:** Software upgrades are finished for the time being after they have been downloaded while the gadget is charging and associated with a Wi-Fi association.

- From a Home screen, explore Settings Icon > General > Software Update.
- Tap Automatic Updates.
- Tap the Automatic Update switch on to allow the auto-updates.

## 2.1 Operating System for iPhone 11

The official iOS 13 launching date was Thursday, September 19, barely three months after the principal beta, in which we got the chance to try out the product early. The iOS 13 discharge date was later than expected. Apple propelled its portable working update on following its new iPhone dispatch occasion, yet this time it gave itself two or three additional days. In any way, you did not need to hold up that long, as the iOS 13 open beta was still out there and had experienced a couple of cycles in the wake of propelling on June 24, 2019.

**iOS 13 enables your Old iPhone to be Quicker, and Long-Lasting**

More individuals are clutching their iPhones for more extended periods, and that is something Apple appears to perceive – and the organization is accelerating iOS 13 to oblige them.

**The Most Significant iOS 13 Details:** application's dispatch speed is up to twice as quick as per Apple, and Face ID opening will be 30% quicker than was previously. Apple likewise figured out how to make application downloads littler, up to 60% by and large; iOS 12 gave us a quicker update, and iOS 13 hopes to expand upon that.

Battery life is likewise something Apple is handling soon. Its point is to slow the pace of battery maturing by lessening the time your iPhone spends when the power is full. iOS 13 should gain from your everyday charging routine so it can hold back to get done with charging past 80% until you have to utilize it.

**Compatibility for iOS 13:** iOS 13 software is perfect with multiple iPhone versions - as far as you hold 6S, SE or some other recent series of iPhone. Indeed, that implies both iPhone 5S as well as 6 do not make the rundown and are always stayed with iOS 12.4.1. However, Apple did not bring any cuts to iOS 12, so it only made up for the lost time during 2019. That sounds reasonable.

**Dark Mode:** Users have been getting the most use out of the iOS 13 elements. It changes up the interface (besides certain outsider applications), trading splendid white and light dim hues for dark and dim shades. That is increasingly lovely on the eyes, particularly around evening time.

**iOS 13 Star Tip:** You can set iOS 13 Dark Mode to switch on and then off at certain occasions, and include it as a Control Center menu alternate way.

**Photograph Altering Devices Get Upgraded:** You would now be able to switch up photographs in 15 unique manners, tweaking features, complexity, and shadows. It is progressively vigorous to where we are opening Adobe Lightroom less.

**iOS 13 Star Tip:** Edits additionally work for video, and you can alter photographs without crushing the Live Photo properties.

**Another QuickPath Console:** Want to swipe on the console as opposed to tap? It is currently in there in iOS 13. No line follows your finger's development, and it is somewhat dubious about becoming acclimated to from the start, yet it is nearer to what we preferred about Gboard.

**iOS 13 Expert Tip:** We discovered this to be generally useful on any huge Max or Plus version iPhone.

**FaceTime Amendment:** Have you ever realized that during FaceTime call you often take a glimpse at your device's screen and hence are not taking a look at camera? Apple would utilize AI for shifting your look's focus point. That might be somehow unwanted on a fundamental level, yet tremendously valuable.

**Face ID has dramatically been Improved:** Users loved this improvement - the area of view to open your phone along with the face is rather extensive. Therefore having a glimpse at the phone on work field would open up your iPhone without having the need to lift your cell phone.

**iOS 13 does Not Go Well with the iPad:** That is nothing but a myth! iOS 13 works equally for iPhone too (iPod Touch also). iPadOS has appeared for iPad along with elite productivity highlights for more significant tablet screen.

**'Discover my iPhone' and 'Discover my Friends' are Melded:** The two apps are presently in a single 'Discover My' application and Apple's inclusive feature that could locate disconnected devices from various iPhones and iPads. The best part is that we would get lesser tracking errors.

**iOS 13 Enhances Battery Life:** That does not signify "time between charges" but the "lifespan of the battery" - the updated iOS 13 version is considerably fast at charging. It would reduce the battery usage at the required occasions. Dark mode would assist as well on iPhone OLED shows.

**Updates Get an Immense (and valuable) Redesign:** An appropriate new structure, Reminders at present take into account better arranging and connections. Probably it would not sound to be such an achievement, yet it is a significant bounce for those who utilize it.

**Camera Got a Significant Overhaul:** Portrait mode (in case your phone bolsters it) would offer increasingly adaptable 'High Key Mono' method and lighting for you to make yourself feel as though you are in a Calvin Klein commercial.

**Siri Sound has also been Enhanced:** A clear voice with increasingly identical lingual control, Siri has been much more user-friendly to talk to now. You probably would not notice it without a next to each other correlation; however, it is here.

**Additional Memoji to have Fun with:** Now you could add make-up, use keyboard to bring in the Memoji stickers - in case you are into your animation face; there is a lot to perform here.

**iOS 13 Master Tip:** Stickers take a shot at iPhone 8 and prior version iPhones, regardless of whether you do not have the TrueDepth camera for shifting Memoji.

**Take Control of Wi-Fi plus Bluetooth More Easily:** Users loved this part: long-press (3D Touch for specific versions of iPhone) on the Bluetooth or Wi-Fi catches in the Control Center. You can get to every one of your associations in a single straightforward spot.

**Use your Phone for the PS4 Remote:** That is right. At present, you could combine your support controller to get the most in a progressively vivid manner. PS4 assistance is here today, while Xbox One help is coming. Ideal for the Apple Arcade, correct?

## Safari

Safari in iOS 13 has a refreshed beginning page that includes your preferred sites, regularly visited websites and most as of late visited sites. It likewise shows significant sites dependent on perusing history, joins sent to you in Messages, and other Siri recommended content. Another View menu in the Smart Search field presents access to message size choices, Reader view, and per-site settings. With per-site settings, you can change the camera, receiver, and area access for each site directly from Safari. It additionally controls the versatile/work area, reader view, and lets you empower content blockers for each site.

While transferring a photograph utilizing Safari, you would now be able to pick little, medium, enormous, and real size alternatives before moving it to decrease picture size whenever wanted. There are new page zoom alternatives, your open tabs can be spared as bookmarks, and you can bounce to an open tab from the pursuit field.

From the Share Sheet in Safari, you would now be able to email a site page as a connection, a PDF, or in peruser view, and with regards to security, there are a couple of new upgrades.

When you attempt to go through a frail secret word when getting paperwork done for a site account, Safari sends a warning, and your Safari history and iCloud-matched up tabs use start to end encryption.

**New HomePod Highlights**

You probably might not have the foggiest idea about this, yet the HomePod is a piece of the iOS community, and it has gotten iOS 13 updates as well. To start with, you can move tunes from your iPhone by essentially holding your phone nearer to the HomePod speaker. Already, you needed to advise Siri to do this; however, now this hand-off element is somewhat simpler.

**The HomePod Likewise Presents Live Radio -** You can ask Siri to play 100,000 stations from all around the globe. Furthermore, HomePod will permit you to perceive who in your family is talking, and customize the reaction - extraordinary with Apple Music, where determinations will be found on your taste and history. It goes past Music, Messages, Notes, Reminders, and then some more elements.

**Apple Sign-In**

Apple is collaborating with Facebook Connect, Google, and different stages that permit you to sign in to outsider records helpfully.

Sign-in with Apple is ready to secure your protection more than Facebook and Google do. What is flawless is that if you would prefer not to surrender your email to an application designer or site, Apple will make an interesting irregular email for you. The email will be novel to that site or application. We are, despite everything, trusting that this will turn out through designers, yet after some time, you will begin seeing it all the more routinely.

**Guides Get Patched Up**

iOS 13 Maps looks much better, regardless of whether everybody likes to loathe on it. Would it be better than Google Maps? Probably yes. For individuals who need Apple's pre-stacked guides application on iOS 13, it is vastly improved. There is far more detail here using Apple revamping maps from the beginning. There is increasingly practical detail for streets, seashores, parks, and structures, and you would now be able to investigate urban areas with a 3D 360-degree experience.

Top picks were a piece of Maps previously, yet iOS 13 makes these spared areas simpler to explore with one tap - they show up at the exceptionally head of a hunt menu. Now and then, Google Maps on iOS does not get this right (however, improves on Android).

That is one motivation to keep Apple Maps introduced, regardless of whether you are a Google Maps individual.

**iOS 13 Highlights Specific for iPhone 11 Series**

- Camera UI catches/wheel switch between ultra-wide and fax
- Holding photograph shade button captures video (no longer for burst photographs)
- The front camera takes wide-point selfies in the scene, 4K60fps video, and 'Selfies'.

There were a couple of new highlights designed for the recently declared iPhone 11 smartphones. As iPhone 11, 11 Pro, and 11 Pro Max are practically about the latest cameras; the iOS 13 programming fits their new ultra-wide focal point and unique night mode. Exchanging between the cameras' focal points (two focal points on iPhone 11 and three on iPhone 11 Pro arrangement) should be consistent, with fast taps or a wheel to change between zoomed-in and zoomed-out viewpoints. Holding down on the natural screen button in iOS 13 beginning account video is much the same as the Snapchat and Instagram UI. Apple asserts that its new handsets offer has been the best video ever in a cell phone, so it is putting a significant accentuation on the fact that it is so natural to shoot video.

On some other iPhone running iOS 13, holding down a similar shade button catches burst photographs.

The front TrueDepth camera on an iPhone 11 phone can catch wide-point selfies when held in the scene direction, and record up to 4K60fps video. Previously, we were denied with 1080p60fps selfie recordings.

Sure to be the fury of everybody more established than millennial age, you are going to begin to see 'Selfies'. This iPhone 11-elite iOS 13 component catches legendary slo-mo video from the front camera.

**Sharing Documents from the iCloud Drive**

With the arrival of iOS 13.4, iPhone clients can at long last offer their iCloud Drive envelopes with other iCloud clients - explicitly utilizing the Files application. Much like Google Docs, they can likewise confine access to either who they unequivocally welcome or give anybody charge, which is connected to the file. They can also pick who makes changes versus just view, just as who can transfer records to the chosen organizer and only download documents.

**Car Keys Assistance**

iOS 13.6, brings support for Car Keys, an element accessible in both the iOS 13 and iOS 14. Vehicle Keys are intended to allow an iPhone or Apple Watch to be utilized instead of an actual key to open an NFC-empowered vehicle. Vehicle Keys should be actualized via vehicle producers to operate, and BMW is one of Apple's first collaborators. BMW's Digital Key for iPhone will let iPhone users tap to open their vehicles, start the vehicle by putting the iPhone in the cell phone plate, place confinements on amateur drivers, and offer keys with up to five multiple users.

In the Health application, there is another "Symptoms" area that lets users include side effects of different diseases, browsing alternatives. For example, body and muscle hurt, hunger changes, hacking, discombobulation, cerebral pain, sickness, and then some more traits.

For the Apple News application, iOS 13.6 includes an element that spares your place in an Apple News article when you begin understanding something and afterward exit out of the article or application, helpful for long-structure content.

Apple News in iOS 13.6 likewise incorporates new Apple News+ Audio highlight where Apple will offer some reports in a sound limit concerning Apple News+ endorsers. There is likewise an everyday sound news recap that is accessible for all Apple News users, just as enhancements to nearby news in certain regions.

**Widespread Purchase**

As of iOS 13.4, app-makers would now be able to select to sell programming over a few or all Apple gadget stages immediately - which means they could purchase an application and have the individual variants opened across iOS, iPadOS, macOS, and tvOS. This element, known as Universal Purchase, is live at this point.

We have talked about some of the traits of iOS 13 software briefly. We shall be discussing them in more detail in Chapter 3, with regards to iPhone 11.

## 2.2 Best Apps for iOS 13

There is amazingly more to 11 and 11 Pro versions of iPhone, and in case you just upgraded, you are most likely wondering about a part of the app you should download to benefit from all they have to offer. Here are some relevant applications for 11 and 11 Pro series of iPhone:

**1. Focos**

In case you like the iPhone's Portrait Mode, you will particularly adore Focos, which allows you to turn back and alter the center after you have taken a picture. It is entirely magnificent. It is generally valuable for representation and still-life snaps, yet you could make several "one of a kind" photographs which dazzle your companions.

**2. Halide**

In case you require a camera app that provides you with more command over presentation, opening, and middle, Halide would be the app. Nevertheless, enabling profundity highlights of iPhone 11 as well as 11 Pro allows you to capture pictures using brilliant RAW for outstanding photos with less advanced commotion.

**3. Canva**

This is a direct and rapid approach for making a schedule for almost anything ranging from a flyer to an Instagram posting or a business card as well. It is free and incredible to deal with vast majority of your primary structure requirements. The paid version makes it easier to disseminate tasks to your circle and lets you approach to an extreme image library so that you could step up the upcoming prompt or web-based post relating to life.

### 4. Adobe Lightroom App

The latest version of Lightroom should not be confused with inheritance variant, i.e. Lightroom Classic. Lightroom is a remarkable executive and altering photograph instrument you could have in the iPhone (or Mac iPad, as far as that is the case). When it has operated in camera, a subscription to Adobe's Creative Cloud results in your device's photograph library to match up over entirety of the gadgets, enabling you to alter images rapidly with the equally helpful assets contained inside your work field.

### 5. LumaFusion

In case you need to alter video with star grade programming, LumaFusion is the best you will jump on iOS. The intensity of the A13 chip in both iPhone 11 as well as 11 Pro makes altering even 4K video basic and quick. It also enables you to import videos from your photo library just as each significant cloud service (a Dropbox, Google Drive, OneDrive) or shared system drives alongside a scope of fare alternatives.

### 6. Dropbox

This one is not only an incredible application for iPhone 11, however for actually any iOS gadget - particularly on the off chance that you need a simple method to keep records synchronized over an assortment of gadgets.

Indeed, many applications do something very similar, yet Dropbox still does it quicker and makes sharing about as straightforward as it gets. It is likewise incredible for rapidly examining in an archive as a PDF and effectively sharing or getting it on your different gadgets.

### 7. Protection Pro

In case you are utilizing any cell phone, a VPN that obstructs the endless number of trackers that unavoidably exist in the applications you use each day is an absolute necessity. Protection Pro permits you to see action and unique square applications or allow them to send information, particularly when running out of sight. It additionally enables you to encode all HTTP associations and even course DNS through VPN.

### 8. Evernote Application

There are certainly optimum unadulterated composing apps (such as, hi, Ulysses). Still, for the multi-reason point to supervise everything including notes and voice reminders, examined records, as well as web clippings. Notably, the hunt feeds (counting OCR that finds archives - including photographs) plus the setting (which raises relevant things) could be beneficial for examination and composing.

**9. Otter.ai**

Consider it like closed subtitling, yet progressive and without the same number of mix-ups. The iPhone application is great, permitting you to record and translate discussions as they occur. You can likewise transfer sound records, and it will deal with the interpretation for you. It even permits you to make gatherings to impart transcripts to your group. The best part is it is free for as long as 600 minutes per month.

**10. Shazam Application**

Apple Inc. possesses the Shazam app. The app can recognize music, films, promoting, and network shows, in light of a short example played and utilizing the amplifier on the gadget. The product is accessible for Windows, macOS, Android, iOS, and watchOS. The application distinguishes tunes dependent on a unique sound mark dependent on a period recurrence diagram known as the spectrogram. It utilizes a cell phone, or PC's worked in receiver to accumulate a short example of a sound playing. Shazam records and organizes a list of sound fingerprints. The user labels a melody for about 10 seconds, while the application makes a sound unique finger impression.

## Are the Apps Not responding on iOS 13?

Once in a while, the applications introduced on iDevice get into mischief arbitrarily. Regardless of what you are attempting to do, it is regular to encounter issues on the iPhone. The problems can be activated because of numerous reasons. What is more, this guide will give the vast majority of the recuperation strategies that you can use to fix when iPhone applications are not taking a shot at iOS 13/13.2.

## What is Going on with your iOS 13/13.2 Applications?

Alongside fixing bugs and presenting new highlights, Apple makes a beta variant accessible with the goal that engineers can prepare their administrations and applications for the last discharge. In this manner, everything implies that there is a likelihood that a portion of the applications introduced on your iPhone would not work appropriately.

## Change iPhone Settings to Fix iOS 13/13.2 Application Issues

The regular changes you should attempt to fix the problems you have been encountering are recorded underneath. We believe that one of them will settle the progressing issue at any rate, and you will have an appropriately working gadget.

### 1. Reset All Settings on iPhone

The primary thought that strikes a chord when the iPhone applications would not open on iOS 13/13.2 is the gadget reset. Typically, it is the settings or similarity issues of the app that interferes with the working. Along these lines, the least demanding thing you should attempt is reestablishing the gadget settings.

**Stage 1:** Launch the Settings application and open General settings. There you will discover the Reset alternative at the base of the rundown.

**Stage 2:** Select the Reset All Settings alternative and affirm the activity by entering your gadget password.

All the settings will be reestablished without erasing the gadget information. You may need to change the settings later as it suits your necessity. However, in any event, the difficulty will be fixed.

### 2. Reset Network Settings

Something else you can attempt if the iPhone applications are smashing on iOS 13/13.2 update is the system settings reset. This reset is utilized when the applications are confronting issues because of system issues. Regardless of whether it is your Wi-Fi or primary availability issue, it tends to be fixed with this technique.

**Stage 1:** Again, get to the Reset menu from the General Settings, and this time, select the Reset Network Settings choice.

**Stage 2:** Enter the password when incited and affirm the reset. It would need a significant period to reestablish the default settings. Remember to reboot your gadget after the reset with the goal that the reset will become active.

### 3. Switch iPhone on and off

The extremely fundamental thing you can attempt when the iPhone applications quit reacting is to power off your iPhone and switch it on afterward. As you are playing out the restart of your gadget, you should follow the correct strides for your device.

### 4. Free up Space of iOS 13/13.2

Mostly when iOS 13/13.2 applications stop responding, it is because the memory space is abandoning your gadget. When the memory is running out, the applications consequently crash, and it must be repaired by exhausting the memory.

**Stage 1:** Open General settings and select the Manage Storage alternative. There you will see the Utilized and Available Space alongside the rundown of applications introduced on your gadget.

**Stage 2:** Select the application which is utilizing the additional memory and erase it from the gadget.

There are such a great number of applications on your iPhone, which you do not use by any means. Erasing such applications will fix the issue, and other significant applications will have enough memory to utilize.

**5. Check Whether Your Device is on Do Not Disturb Mode**

Often, the users do not understand that the "Don't Disturb" mode is enabled. When this mode is on, the users imagine that their iPhone applications have quit reacting. So, look at whether the mode is on or off and afterward try utilizing the app in question.

## 2.3 iOS 13 Accessibility

iOS 13 has been with us for a long while now, and we trust Apple will introduce again a considerable amount of new availability highlights and enhancements accompanying iOS 14. We all are much aware of the importance of accessibility for Apple. A year ago, new highlights and accessibility were one of the center themes they canvassed in the Platforms State of the Union meeting.

The main thing they discussed was Discoverability. Apple truly needs everybody to utilize any of their gadgets directly out of the container, so they made conceivable to design your openness inclinations on iOS' Quick Start onboarding process. What is more, they likewise moved accessibility to the high degree of Settings, so it gives it permeability, and it makes it simpler to discover.

This part of the chapter will mainly highlight the upgrades relating to accessibility: explicitly, those progressions which affect people who are visually impaired, deaf, or both

**Voice Control**

Voice Control feature won the show at the Union Meeting. Apple introduced this new component that lets you utilize your gadget with a progression of voice orders. You will presumably think what the point of VoiceOver is when there is already Siri. In any case, Voice Control is an increasingly nonexclusive feature that lets you interface with any piece of the framework and with any application you have introduced. More significantly, it runs completely on-gadget, so it will work regardless of whether you are disconnected.

You can allude to things in the screen by name, by number, or utilizing a matrix-based format for better control. You can alter text, and you can talk motions. It uses the camera to check on the off chance you are addressing the gadget or if you are looking elsewhere. It works like enchantment!

On the off chance that your application underpins VoiceOver well, the odds are that it will be genuinely acceptable with Voice Control.

Voice Control is an extraordinary path for testing your applications for availability. Open your app, go to a screen you need to test, and state "Show names". Voice Control will overlay all of the accessibility marks you have designed. This is a fast method to check whether they are complete or if there are any absent.

How could you support the Voice Control further? In case your application has accessibility, you will see that it works very well. However, the accessibility marks you have designed probably might not be the best for Voice Control. This can be because you may need them to be shorter and more straightforward. Or then again, to make it more intuitive, you might need to give various options of what the user can say so they do not need to recall a particular name.

### The Most Effective Method to set up the Accessibility Shortcut

- Open the Settings application.
- In the Settings application, select accessibility from the rundown.
- On the Accessibility screen, look to the base and select Accessibility Shortcut.
- The following screen would record all the highlights you can dole out to the Accessibility Shortcut. Select all the highlights you might want the alternate way to initiate.

### Utilizing the Accessibility Shortcut

- Triple-click the Home option on gadgets that have a Home option. Triple-click the Side option on devices that utilize Face ID.
- In case you just doled out one element to the Accessibility Shortcut, it will open straight mindful. Triple-click the option again so that it would be disabled.
- In case you doled out numerous highlights to the Accessibility Shortcut, select from the rundown.

### Avail the Control Centre Option

You can, likewise, get the Accessibility Shortcut from the Control Center.

- **To utilize Control Center:** Go to Settings > Control Center > Customize Controls, at that point tap close to availability highlights, for example, Accessibility Shortcuts, Magnifier, Hearing Aids, and Guided Access.
- **To actuate an accessibility highlight from Control Center:** Open Control Center, at that point, tap accessibility feature.

**VoiceOver**

**Haptics and Sounds**

One of the critical things you may see upon the fruitful establishment of iOS 13 is that your iPhone will begin clicking and giving you other material input. Something else you may quickly notice is that there exist updated VoiceOver sounds.

In case the sounds or haptics are not something you are appreciating, you can change these settings by visiting the Settings > Accessibility > VoiceOver > Audio > Sounds and Haptics. In this menu, you have the alternative to turn both sounds and haptics on or off. You can likewise browse one of 3 power levels of the haptic input. You cannot just flip these alternatives on and off, yet can also pick which sounds are heard, or haptics are felt.

If you need any criticism from both of these settings, you should turn them on, and afterward, turn the entirety of the sounds and haptics you do not wish to use off.

**Easier Scrolling**

Most screens, with VoiceOver allowed, will presently show what is known as a "vertical bar for scrolling". The motivation behind this parchment bar is to have the option to rapidly move to various pieces of records, messages, books, and so forth. You will typically discover it on the right side of your touchscreen. When VoiceOver talks or shows a "vertical scrolling bar," you will likewise find that you are on a particular page with a percentage given too. These let you know how far down in the content you are. For instance, if you are at 99%, you will be close to the base of the content shown. Scrolling all over will handle how far down you are in the material. If you flip up with one finger to half and flick left at that point, you will be part of the way through the rundown of things on that page.

**Simpler to Capture Pictures**

When taking photographs in the Camera application, VoiceOver would now provide you much more insights to assist you with getting the image you need.

VoiceOver will demonstrate the degree of the camera and portray the area of individuals in the view discoverer. For instance, if your camera is inclined 15 degrees to one side, it will tell you this. In the event when one individual is in the base right of the view discoverer, this data will likewise be voiced. Further, VoiceOver can recognize who the individual is in the view discoverer if it is known in your photo library. At last, iOS would endeavor to distinguish the first item in the scene. This is one case where AI and machine learning have met up to make this assignment a lot simpler for users who are visually impaired.

Apple keeps on making changes and improvements to its versatile working framework for everybody. Their work toward comprehensive plan lets them take the lead ahead of various other forums and platforms, particularly regarding the accessibility upgrades; evidently, the enhancements in iOS 13 demonstrate that this pattern shall proceed. Much the same as past iOS launches, whether you should update or not relies upon whether the bugs present in the new start will affect you on a more exceptional level than you can endure—and whether you feel the new highlights merit the redesign. On the other hand, it might be ideal to evaluate iOS 13 on another gadget before using it.

## Backing up the Device with iOS 13

Through iOS 13, the 5s and six versions of iPhone are not supported anymore. So in case you own an iOS gadget that is more up to date compared to iPhone 6, there may be the option to get iOS 13 software. You ought to consistently remember that it would be wise to back-up your gadget when you modified your gadget. By backing up your iOS 13 device, you will never be deprived of any information.

Regarding backing up an iOS gadget, the principal strategy you may recollect is iTunes or iCloud. For sure, they are one of the widely recognized approaches for backing-up and reestablishing the iOS device. In any case, regardless of iCloud or iTunes, both have their restrictions. Is there some other alternative for backing-up your iPad or iPhone on the off chance that you do not care for utilizing iCloud and iTunes? Also, this portion of the chapter would fundamentally encourage you towards the back-up of your iPad or iPhone without using iCloud or iTunes, once the iOS 13 software has been updated.

## The Most Effective Method for iPhone Backup without iTunes

For backing-up your iOS gadget without utilizing iCloud or the iTunes, we earnestly prescribe you an apparatus, i.e.

Syncios Data Transfer. This tool is an expert utility intended for making a back-up of cell phones. It permits you a specifically back-up content contrasted to iTunes that renders complete back-up. Furthermore, when you reestablish information from iTunes back-up, it will delete every current datum, whereas Syncios Data Transfer would not. So basically, download and introduce Syncios Data Transfer for backing-up Contacts, Photos, Messages, digital books, Notes, Videos, Call logs, Music, and other components to PC. The means are beneath:

**Stage 1: Install as well as Release Syncios Tool**

You can free download plus introduce the incredible back-up device. The two Windows forms and Mac adaptation are accessible; simply choose and then download the good one into your PC, and enable it.

**Stage 2: Link your iPad or iPhone with Mac or PC**

You would have three modes accessible on the primary interface. To back-up, your iOS gadget, click on the Back-up method on the board, interface the iOS 13 gadget to Mac or PC with a USB link, and click on the "Next" option to continue.

Select your ideal information; for example, Messages, Contacts, Music and Photos, on the board, Syncios would stack the information. Consequently, it might require some time, as indicated by the amount of your material.

**Stage 3: Start Backing-Up your iOS Gadget**

After selecting every ideal material, select the "Next" option to begin the back-up procedure. Sooner or later, the entirety of your chosen information would be upheld on your PC effectively. You are permitted to reestablish back-up records on your iOS 13 idevice, at whatever point you need.

In the beta form, we face the challenge of losing information when our gadget is running it. It is astute to back-up your idevice generally on the off chance that something turns out badly and brought about information misfortune. With the Syncios Tool, you could easily back up the gadget to PC quickly and reestablish the back-up to the device whenever you need it. When you do not care for the iTunes, Syncios Data Tool could be the effective option.

# Chapter 3: iPhone 11- Features and Specifications

iPhone 11 is a cell phone planned, created, and promoted by Apple Inc. It is the thirteenth era less-costly iPhone, succeeding the iPhone XR. It was divulged on September 10, 2019.

The conspicuous changes compared to iPhone XR is the Apple A13 Bionic chip and an ultra-wide double camera framework. While the iPhone 11 Pro accompanies an 18 W Lightning to USB-C quick charger, the iPhone 11 accompanies a similar 5W charger found on past iPhones.

iPhone 11 is accessible in six hues: Yellow, Purple, Green, White, Product (Red), and Black. There is a score at the front for the TrueDepth camera framework and speaker, like its antecedent, iPhone XR. There is a knock in the back for the cameras and the blaze that is a similar size as iPhone 11 Pro, even though iPhone 11 just has two cameras contrasted with the Pro's three cameras. Additionally, iPhone 11 has a matte glass back camera lodging and gleaming glass back, while iPhone 11 Pro has a reflexive glass back camera lodging and matte glass back. The Apple logo is presently fixated on the rear of the gadget with no content, a change from past models.

Many features of iPhone 11 have already been discussed in the previous chapter, relating to iOS 13 software; some more prominent ones would be discussed here.

## 3.1 Prominent Features and their Functionality

iPhone 11, alongside iPhone 11 Pro, utilizes Apple's A13 Bionic processor, which contains a third-age neural motor. It has three inside stockpiling choices: 64 GB, 128 GB, and 256GB. It additionally has 4 GB of RAM. iPhone 11 has an IP68 water and residue safe rating alongside soil and grime and is water-safe up to two meters for 30 minutes. In any case, the maker guarantee does not cover fluid harm to the phone. Additionally, as past iPhones, these phones do not have an earphone jack and accompany wired EarPods with a Lightning connector. iPhone 11 is the first cell phone with worked in ultra-wideband equipment, through its Apple U1 chip.

iPhone 11 has a 6.1 in (15.5 cm) IPS LCD, unlike the Pro models, which have OLED shows. The goal is 1792 × 828 pixels (1.5 megapixels at 326 ppi) with a most extreme splendor of 625 nits and a 1400:1 differentiation proportion. It bolsters Dolby Vision, HDR10, True-Tone, and wide shading extent.

Similarly, as with iPhone 11 Pro, XR, XS, and X, the showcase has a point at the top for the TrueDepth camera structure and the speaker. The showcase has an oleophobic covering that is a unique finger impression resistant. Apple reported in September 2019 that both iPhone 11 and iPhone 11 Pro would show an admonition notice if a presentation were supplanted with an unapproved part. Apple expressed that issues with the telephone could emerge if inappropriate components or systems were utilized during the fix procedure.

**Camera**

iPhone 11 incorporates a double focal point 12 MP back camera exhibit. There is one *f*/2.4 ultra-wide point focal point with a 120-degree field of view and 2× optical zoom out and one *f*/1.8 wide edge focal point. iPhone 11 backings 4K video at up to 60 fps and 1080p moderate movement at up to 240 fps. The phone likewise includes a sound zoom highlight, which centers sound on the territory that is being focused on, like the Pro model.

With iOS 13, iPhone 11 presently can take shots at 16:9. Already, you could just alter a photograph to that proportion sometime later – and, after it is all said and done, it was only a yield work.

The element is, in reality, somewhat covered up in the Camera application, as well. You will have to play out a slide and tap with your finger to get to the shrouded camera proportion modes.

Both of the cameras bolster video, albeit, just the essential focal point has OIS. It supports a Portrait Mode with profundity control and a progressed Bokeh impact. The phone likewise has a programmed Night Mode permitting the camera to take more beautiful pictures with diminished clamor in low light situations.

Likewise, there is an updated camera app that involves new highlights, for instance, a parchment wheel for picking between the multiple focal points and an element called "QuickTake" which permits the client to long-press the shade catch to take a video. Apple has likewise reported another Deep Fusion to include which exploits AI for picture preparing and was discharged through iOS 13.2 programming update on October 29.

Details about QuickTake and Deep Fusion features have been included in more detail in Chapter 4.

**Programming**

iPhone 11 comes with iOS 13, which incorporates Face ID (through the TrueDepth camera), Siri, Apple Pay, and supports Apple Card. It will be perfect with iOS 14 in fall 2020.

## The UI Chip

One of the most noteworthy inside augmentations to the latest iPhone 11 is the U1 chip. All the new iPhones have it inside. This chip powers ultra-wideband innovation. Set forth plainly, this innovation can pinpoint the area of things like a phone or a tracing tag. It could even be employed to open your vehicle. By assuming how long it takes for pulses of short radio to move between the gadgets, it figures out exact areas for your lost things. Using the U1 chip, you could ping a tag from your phone to find the item inside your home.

There is just a single authority use case for the U1 chip: improved AirDrop exactness in iOS 13. Once in a while, when utilizing AirDrop, it can require some investment to discover the individual you are attempting to move to, mainly if there are a ton of other AirDrop users. With the U1 chip, you will have the option to direct the iPhone to another iPhone to manage the exchange. This innovation has a tremendous potential past increasingly proficient AirDrops. Suppose that you were approaching your vehicle on the off chance, it could perceive your phone and open. Or on the contrary, your PC could wake from rest when you went into the room.

### Custom Corning Glass

Consistently during its September keynote, Apple says its glass is the hardest ever in a cell phone. It has primarily been crafted by Corning, the organization behind Gorilla Glass. While this is not immense amazement given that Corning has provided the glass for each iPhone since 2007, Apple made its subsequent interest in Corning for future improvement of iPhone, Apple Watch, and iPad glass. Gorilla Glass 6 is the most recent adaptation of Corning's extreme glass, which has likewise been utilized on other leader phones recently, for example, the Galaxy Note 10 Plus. As indicated by the organization's particulars, Gorilla Glass 6 can endure 15 drops from a tallness of 3.2 feet (1 meter). The Gorilla glass is explicit to Apple. The glass is altogether harder than anticipated.

### The Siri Application

Siri is a worked-in "insightful aide" that empowers those using iOS gadgets to talk voice orders to operate the cell phone and its applications. She is accessible on iPhone 4s or later, iPad Pro, iPad (third era or later), iPad Air or later, iPad smaller than usual or later, and iPod contact (fifth era or later) and requires internet to work.

Users could talk orders, get discernible affirmation from Siri, send messages, place calls, set updates, work iTunes, and the sky is the limit.

Siri sounds clearer than any time in recent memory, especially while talking more extended expressions, with a voice produced entirely by programming. Siri offers customized recommendations in Apple Podcasts, Maps, and Safari. Siri can even differentiate between updates in messages and occasions in outsider applications. Siri would now have the control to play music, digital broadcasts, book recordings, and radio with outsider apps. Request Siri to check out your preferred radio broadcast.

"Hello Siri" is bolstered on iPhone SE, iPhone 6s or later, iPad Pro (aside from 12.9-inch, first era), and iPad (fifth era or later) without being connected to power. "Hello Siri" is bolstered on iPhone, iPad, and iPod contact with iOS 8 or later while connected. It is not upheld on the first-generation iPad, iPad 2, and first-generation (mini) iPad.

**1. Setting up Hey Siri**

- Set up the Settings application on your iOS gadget.
- Look down and select Siri and Search.

- Empower Listen for Hey Siri.
- Tap Enable Siri.
- Siri will request that you train her. Tap Continue.
- State "Hello Siri" into the gadget.
- When Siri has the data she needs, you would see a checkmark.
- State "Hello Siri, how is the climate today?"
- Then state, "Hello Siri, it is me."
- Hello, Siri is then prepared.

**2. Enabling Siri**

- Get the Settings application on your iOS gadget.
- Look down and select Siri and Search.
- Pick whether to empower Siri by voice with Hey Siri or decide to press the catch for Siri simply.
- Tap Enable Siri.

**3. Changing Siri's Language**

- From your Siri settings screen, tap Language and select your favored Language.

**4. Securing Siri's Lock Screen**

From your Siri settings screen, slide the Access on Lock Screen catch to green. This will permit you to address Siri through your Lock Screen. However, this could bring down the security of your gadget.

**5. Changing Siri's Voice**

- From your Siri settings screen, tap Siri Voice and select the voice you would like.

## Health Application

### Summary

In iOS 13, Apple upgraded the Health application, getting rid of the iOS 12 interface, which included four tabs for the Health Data, Today Calendar, and Medical ID and Sources.

The principle Health interface presently includes only two tabs: Summary and Browse.

The summary is a review of the entirety of your distinctive wellbeing measurements, which will shift depending on what wellbeing related gadgets you have and how you use them.

In case you have an Apple Watch, you will see information like pulse, action, pulse fluctuation, stand minutes, stand hours, steps, and more.

Different gadgets, similar to the smart scales, Beddit monitor for sleep, Blood pressure screens, and others associated with the Health application, could likewise be shown here. To alter the contents of "Summary Tab," click on "Edit" catch and press stars close to the classes that you need to see.

## Highlights Section

There is a "Highlights" segment in the "Summary" tab, which reveals essential and fascinating data that you should know. The data includes: usual exercise minutes in the course of the most recent seven days, pulse recuperation, general steps strolled every day, ecological sound levels, and some more.

## Bring Health App to Greater Use

If you look down to the furthest limit of the Summary segment in the Health application, you will see different choices like enrolling as an organ giver, alongside wellbeing related data, for example, why hearing wellbeing matters and understanding hearing misfortune. There are additional connections to wellbeing related applications for you to try.

## Browse Tab

"Browse" tab of the Health application would provide you with a breakdown of the entirety of the available well-being-related classes.

The aim is to render it easier to discover diverse wellbeing data and your wellbeing records if you have a specialist's office that makes records accessible on the iPhone. This segment likewise incorporates the search category so you could scan for precisely what you are searching for.

### Profile

Data like Sources and Medical ID, which was already accessible through committed tabs in the iOS 12 Health application, is presently situated in another Profile segment available by tapping on your profile picture at the head of the Health application.

Your wellbeing subtleties (weight, height, age, and so forth) are put away here, alongside your Medical ID data and decisions regarding your organ donations. In this segment, you can likewise get to your wellbeing records on the off chance that you have a performing health supplier. You could change which applications and gadgets might approach your Health information.

### Breakdowns for Health Data

Since the Health application is not, at this point, sorted out by date, it appears to be unique when you tap into a wellbeing classification such as steps taken or practice minutes.

You could even observe information composed by day, week, month, or year. It is simpler to discover every class that you are searching for, and Apple likewise gives helpful wellbeing synopses in these segments. Contingent upon the wellbeing classification, measurements like daily average, historical average, alerts, range, and much more are also accessible.

**Monitoring Noise**

iOS 13 screens the sound level around you through associated earbuds like the AirPods, EarPods, Powerbeats Pro, and different alternatives. The Health application can be set to send notices when destructive clamor levels are recognized; for example, if you are at a show that is excessively noisy or tuning in to music through the AirPods or different earphones, that is set excessively uproarious.

In the Health application explicitly, Apple gives a readout of the encompassing commotion you presented to. The app informs you whether it has been excessively boisterous and gives the average sound level in your condition in the most recent hour, day, week, month, and year.

### Toothbrushing Hours

In case you have a Bluetooth-associated toothbrush that works with an iPhone application, that information would now be brought into the Health application in another Toothbrushing class so you could see your brushing time initially. The Toothbrushing class tracks brushing time every day, week, month, and year. In case you do not hold a Bluetooth-empowered toothbrush, you could likewise include manual information each time that you brush your teeth.

### Activity Application

iOS 13's Activity app has another "Trends" tab intended to ensure you keep up your movement levels from month to month. Trends informs you whether your general wellbeing patterns are steady, up, or down, so if the activity range has dropped, you could roll out the proper improvements.

To give you a report about your progress, Trends goes through or down bolts. An up bolt implies your movement in a particular class is up, while a sliding bolt means you are drifting downwards.

Move (calories through dynamic development every day), Stand hours, Exercise minutes, and Distance strolled, and, contingent upon which exercises you perform, are covered by the Trends. Measurements like Stand Minutes out of every Hour, VO2MAX, Walking Pace, and Running Pace are likewise accessible. However, you need enough information to enact them. These depend on strolling and running exercises.

Apple says that Trends is intended to assist users with an understanding of long-term activity path, portability, and wellness through the span of the most recent 90 days. Tapping on any of the bolts in the Trends tab gives increasingly explicit data so you could observe changes after some time in more detail. Apple will provide you with an empowering message if your patterns move upward or customized instructing if trends move down.

**iCloud Drive**

iCloud Drive is a piece of iCloud; Apple's distributed storage administration that propelled in 2011.

It lets you spare photographs, recordings, reports, music, and application information to iCloud. It even permits you to make new records and organizers from iCloud-empowered applications and work on similar documents over different forms. You can store any kind of record in iCloud Drive if it is under 50GB in size.

The moment you follow iCloud, you are bestowed with 5GB free stockpiling for Mail, Backup, and iCloud Drive. You could reestablish the iCloud stockpiling schedule from your iPad, iPhone, iPod contact, Mac, or PC whenever required. Simply browse a total of 2TB, 200GB or 50GB.

In addition to the fact that it lets you store all your stuff in one spot, iCloud Drive enables you to get to the entirety of your documents and information from your iOS gadget, Mac, and Windows PC. You could afterward keep those records and organizers updated over the whole of your devices. Before you set up iCloud Drive, ensure your iOS gadget is running iOS 13 or subsequent version.

**Turn on iCloud Drive**

After you set up iCloud Drive, any reports that you have just put away in iCloud will consequently be moved to iCloud Drive.

In case you do not see your documents for the stored applications, they may be on a gadget that does not have iCloud Drive turned on - so make sure to allow it on all your devices.

- Visit Settings, and Your Name.
- Tap iCloud.
- Turn on iCloud Drive.

You can discover your iCloud Drive records in the File application. To get to your records, simply open the Files application and pick the area of the document you are searching for. It is anything but difficult to organize the File application, and when you make changes on one gadget, such alterations are consequently refreshed on each gadget utilizing iCloud Drive.

You could also make your envelopes. Or on the other hand, rename envelopes you as of now have, and you can spare and move iCloud Drive documents in the middle of organizers. Need to impart data to a companion or partner? You can share any envelope or record put away in iCloud Drive straightforwardly from the Files application, as well.

**Audio Zoom Feature**

Recording a subject talking in a packed domain can be hard.

Be that as it may, Phone 11 currently has a component that can enable you "to center" your gadget's amplifiers for more transparent sound. A comparative element initially sprung up on Samsung gadgets; however, it is presently in Apple's most recent handsets. The element is, suitably, called Audio Zoom. What is more, it works about how you anticipate. When you focus on a matter, the iPhone will "center" the amplifiers regarding that matter while "obscuring" out commotion from different directions. It chips away at everything from individuals conversing with machines making a clamor.

**Wi-Fi 6**

Though numerous other phone makers are scrambling to actualize some sort of 5G support in their most recent handsets, Apple discreetly redesigned another network choice on its iPhone 11 and iPhone 11 Pro models. With Wi-Fi 6, anticipate better execution in jam-packed regions, improved information speeds, and other massive overhauls.

**Steadiness Detection Feature**

iPhone 11 will have the option to recognize whether it is consistent.

Mostly, if you have it mounted on a tripod or inclining toward something, it will have the option to know.

When it does, it will give you extra-long presentation choices, letting you set introduction times as long as 10 seconds. That is a shelter for Night Mode yet in addition to a wide scope of other photographic strategies.

**Catch Outside the Frame**

One of the cleverest, however, lesser-known highlights in iPhone 11 is called Capture Outside the Frame. It will consequently spare extra picture space around your image. It resembles a different yield, letting you include a greater picture, once more into a shot, after you have taken it. Another related element called Auto-Apply makes it a stride further. The framework will identify whether an individual's face is cut off in a picture and will naturally "de-crop" and expand the frame's edges to include that individual's face back in. That is a distinct advantage.

**SF Camera Text Style**

Inside the new iPhone 11, there is the typeface element in one single application. We are referring to the unique SF Camera textual style that Apple has actualized in the latest gadgets. Except if you are quirky about typefaces, you likely will not give it a second thought or notice.

In any case, SF Camera is a well-planned typeface with a somewhat increasingly modern look. Furthermore, once more, Apple just uses it in the Camera application.

**Find My Application**

Before you can locate a lost gadget, discover loved ones, and share your area, you have to set up Find My. After you set up Find My application, you can find a lost or taken gadget, or even assist a companion locate their missing device. Likewise, you can impart your area specifications to companions, family, and contacts, request to follow a companion's area or get bearings to a companion's area.

**Enable Find My for your iPhone 11**

- On your iPhone 11, open the Settings application.
- Select your name.
- Click Find My.
- On the off chance that you require closed ones to know where you are, turn on Share My Location.
- Press Find My [device], at that point switch, Find My [device] on.

To see your gadget in any event, when it is disconnected, turn on Enable Offline Finding. To have the area of your device sent to Apple when the battery is low, turn on Send Last Location.

In case you need to have the option to locate your lost gadget on a guide, ensure that Location Services is turned on. To do this, move to Settings, select Privacy, then Location Services, and turn on the spot benefits.

**Display Notification Aftermarket**

At times, phones end up with broken screens. What is more, in some cases, the proprietors of those phones consult the outsider fix shops that will trade the showcase glass with a low-quality product. Much of the time, these screens can bring about more unfortunate touch and display execution. That can be an issue in case you are purchasing a utilized iPhone on a commercial center application.

Fortunately, in the iPhone 11, Apple has executed another arrangement to distinguish and notify users about repairs for the display. You would now be able to check whether an iPhone 11 has a non-real, reseller's exchange display just by visiting Settings, then selecting General, and then About.

**Audio Books**

Keeping in mind that there are bundles of value outsider applications out there for tuning in to book recordings, the iPhone 11's exclusive book recording stage, Apple Books, is a commendable application.

In case you are prepared to include more than music and digital recordings to your iPhone's sound arrangement, here are how to begin downloading and tuning in to book recordings in the Apple Books application.

1. Open up Apple Books application on your iPhone. In the case that you have never utilized it and are not sure where it lives on your iPhone, swipe directly from the center of the screen to pull up the hunt bar.

2. Select "Audio Books" from the menu at the base of the screen. You can likewise tap "Explore Audiobooks" from the "Reading Now" tab, which is the page that opens whenever you dispatch the application, to be taken to a similar page.

3. You can discover a book recording by investigating classes, as "New and Trending," the top graphing book recordings, or unique value bargains.

4. Assuming in any case, you recognize what book recording you would prefer to download, go directly to the "Search" tab, on the extreme right, and type in the name.

5. Tap the book that you would prefer to tune in to, ensuring the title is under the "Book recordings" class.

6. You can decide to review the book, endow it, or even add it to a list of things to get. In case you are prepared to purchase, tap the dark "Purchase" button, which will incorporate the book recording cost.

7. For the most part, the book will begin downloading promptly on the off chance that you are associated with Wi-Fi. Press "Listen" to start listening immediately.

8. When you need to return to the book recording later, you can discover it in "Library" inside Apple Books.

**Double SIM Support**

Double SIM support, which permits two phone numbers to be utilized at once, is being used for iPhone 11. Double SIM usefulness is empowered through the consideration of one physical nano-SIM space and an eSIM. The eSIM is accessible in numerous nations around the globe, and Apple has a full rundown of transporters that help eSIM on its site. Double SIMs work with select transporters in Canada, Austria, Croatia, Germany, Czech Republic, Hungary, Spain, India, the United States, and the UK.

**Face ID Security and Privacy**

Face ID utilizes a nitty-gritty 3D facial output that cannot be tricked by a photograph, veil, or other facial impersonation.

A "Consideration Aware" security highlight permits Face ID to open your gadget when you look towards the iPhone 11 with your eyes open. Therefore, it does not work when your eyes are shut when you are resting when you are oblivious or are turning away from your phone.

Consideration mindful is discretionary, and there is an availability highlight to turn it off for the individuals who cannot concentrate on the iPhone's screen. However, a great many people should leave it turned on for the additional layer of security. With the consideration mindful element, the iPhone 11 realizes when you are taking a gander at it. Face ID shows warnings and messages on the Lock screen when you take a gander at iPhone 11; it makes the screen lit. It consequently brings down the volume of an alert or ringer when it realizes your consideration is on the iPhone 11's presentation.

If a hoodlum requests your iPhone, Face ID can be disabled rapidly and discretely by pushing as an afterthought button and the volume button simultaneously. Do this before giving your phone over, and a hoodlum would not have the option to filter your face. Face ID likewise kills after two bombed facial acknowledgment endeavors, and a password should be entered for it to be walked out on.

Face ID information is scrambled and put away in the Secure Enclave on the iPhone 11. Apple cannot get to your Face ID information, nor can any individual who has your phone. Confirmation happens totally on your gadget, with no Face ID information at any point put away in the cloud or transferred to Apple. Outsider engineers do not approach the facial guide that Face ID uses to open a gadget. The TrueDepth camera can be utilized to check a user's face to make increasingly reasonable expanded reality applications.

With Face ID, there is a 1 out of 1,000,000 possibility that another person's face can trick Face ID, yet the deceit rate increases to 1 out of 500,000 with a substitute appearance enrolled in iOS 13. Face ID has been deceived by indistinguishable twins, kids, and a deliberately made cover. Yet, despite everything secure enough, the average individual should not stress over their iPhone being opened by another person.

**AirPods**

Siri can peruse approaching notices from your informing applications to your second-generation AirPods when you cannot go after your phone. Pair two arrangements of AirPods to one iPhone and appreciate a similar tune or film alongside a companion.

## Messages and Memoji

### Offer Name along with Photograph

Share your photograph and name while you start discussion or while the other person gives reaction in message. Select whether you want to share with everyone, only with your contacts, or with no one. You could even decide to utilize a picture, an Animoji, or a monogram for the photo image.

### Memoji Stickers

Consequently, create sticker bundles based upon your Animoji and Memoji characters that permit you to communicate your feelings through Messages.

### Enhanced Search

Searching in Messages renders it simpler to figure out what you are searching for. In fact, even before a character is typed, you could detect late messages, photographs, individuals, connections, as well as areas which you may be searching for. At the point when a search is typed in, Messages application classifies the features and outcomes coordinating terms.

### Enhanced Details Pane

Details Pane composes connections and areas which have been included in discussion, so they are anything but hard to track down initially.

### Enhanced Memoji Customization Feature

Cosmetics lets you tweak redden and eyeshadow as well as incorporate altering apparatuses that simplify the perfect look. Tweak your teeth using braces or add piercings to your eyebrows, nose, eyelids, and around the mouth area. There are additionally 30 new hairdos, above 15 new bits of headwear, plus the additional glasses and studs.

### Latest Animoji

Three additional Animoji characters —dairy animals, octopus and mouse — grant you more options to communicate.

### Hardware Support for Animoji

All the devices having A9 chip (subsequent models as well) support Animoji and Memoji sticker packs.

## 3.2 iPhone 11- Battery and Charging

iPhone 11 has a 3,110mAH battery. Whereas it accompanies the 5W charger inside the Apple's case. The limit is successfully served when contrasted with the 6S version, which is why charging can get twice as long as you utilize the equivalent 5W charger.

iPhone 11 has a glass body with worked in remote charging curls to help remote charging usefulness. Apple uses the Qi remote charging standard that is additionally accessible in many Android phones, which implies the new iPhones can accuse remotely of any Qi-confirmed inductive charger. iPhone 11 works with 7.5W and 5W remote charging frill; however, 7.5W charging is quicker. Various organizations have now evolved remote charging alternatives structured explicitly for Apple's iPhones. Some 7.5W chargers are done charging at 5W on iPhone 11 and 11 Pro, which is essential for anybody considering making a remote charger buy.

The wise option is to purchase Apple's charger that is an 18W USB-C along with Lightning to the USB-C wire. These are similar accessories that are included with 11 Pro and 11 Pro Max versions of iPhone. The higher-appraised power connector implies you could charge your iPhone 11 much quicker. With USB-C block, you would fast charge going from the 0% to about 50% in around 30 minutes. The complete charge to the 100% would need about 90 minutes.

In case you would prefer not to switch to USB-C power connector world yet, you could at present charge all the more rapidly by utilizing the older-version iPad chargers.

They are the 12W chargers, and while they are not exactly as quick as 18W alternative, they will even now be fundamentally quicker than 5W block.

### Hybrid Power Control

Apple's iPhone power control frameworks certainly have unfavorable criticism. Your iPhone's battery is going to corrupt in the long run and cause sudden shutdowns or more unfortunate execution. Apple has concocted another approach to battle that in iPhone 11. The organization's 2019 record of iPhones has an updated programming equipment framework that should moderate the effects of battery debasement.

### Optimizing Battery Charging

This feature is not confined to iPhone 11 or 11 Pro; instead, it is a component remembered for iOS 13. Improved Battery Charging learns your daily charging propensities, utilizing any set cautions in the Clock application, appropriately charging your iPhone's battery every night, and lessening the sum it debases after some time.

All the more explicitly, your iPhone will quickly charge to 80% when you plug it in or place it on a wireless charger.

When it gets to 80%, the battery will remain there until you wake up, after which it will continue charging to 100%. The final product is a more advantageous charging cycle for your phone's battery and a battery that will last more.

Turn on Battery Optimization in Settings, battery, then visit Battery Health and then press Optimized Battery Charging.

## 3.3 Price Specifications of iPhone 11

The iPhone 11 retails for $699 (about $29 every month utilizing Apple's financing plan). Contrasted with iPhone XR, which appeared in 2018 for $749, and iPhone XS, which cost $999, is astounding; however, it is great news. The cost is even lower on the off chance that you have a past model iPhone to exchange. Apple is presenting to $600 off on the new iPhone 11 on the off chance that you have an iPhone XS Max, making the buy just $100. Comparatively, the two new leaders, iPhone 11 Pro and Pro Max, began at $999 and $1,099.

## 3.4 iPhone 11 Repair Policy

If your iPhone 11's issue is secured by the Apple guarantee, an AppleCare plan, or shopper law, there is no charge. This does exclude unplanned harm, which requires an expense.

Assuming that your iPhone has unplanned harm and you have AppleCare+ inclusion, you can utilize one of your coincidental harm episodes to cover the fix. Every occurrence of unforeseen harm inclusion is dependent upon an AppleCare+ administration expense or a deductible, contingent upon your arrangement. In case your iPhone was harmed, and you do not have an AppleCare+ inclusion, your fix charge will differ, contingent upon the fix. These out-of-guarantee costs are for fixes made by Apple. Apple Authorized Service Providers may include their expenses. According to Apple's arrangement, iPhone 11's screen fix with no guarantee would cost around $199.

**Arrange a Fix**

Arrange to bring your iPhone 11 into an Apple Authorized Service Provider or the Genius Bar. Arrange nearby help to have an Apple Authorized Service Provider go to your home or office to finish your gadget fix. On location, the administration is accessible in select areas and has an extra site-visit charge. This additional expense will be postponed if AppleCare+ secures your iPhone.

**Send in for Fix**

At the point when you organize to send in your iPhone 11 for a fix, Apple shall send you a crate with pre-printed marks to gather your iPhone, and afterward, you can transport it to an Apple Repair Center whenever the timing is ideal. Each Apple fix with an Apple Authorized Service Provider, the Genius Bar, or an Apple Repair Center is performed by an Apple-prepared expert utilizing Apple exactness apparatuses. They convey top-notch administration using just authentic Apple parts, and Apple will uphold your fix.

AppleCare+ with Theft and Loss incorporates up to two occurrences of unplanned harm, robbery, or misfortune inclusion every 24 months. Each episode is dependent upon the deductibles. For iPhone 11, the fee would be around $ 229. Likewise, you will get Express Replacement Service, and every minute of every day needs access to Apple specialists by a visitor through the phone service.

Robbery and misfortune inclusion expects you to have to "Find My" iPhone empowered on your gadget when it is lost or taken.

**How to insure iPhone 11?**

- Buy AppleCare+ with your latest iPhone 11.

- Or on the other hand, get it during 60 days of your iPhone buy:

On your gadget (Visit Settings, select General, select About and pick AppleCare+ Coverage Available)

- On the web (expects you to confirm your sequential number and run a far off analytic)

At an Apple Store (investigation of iPhone and verification of procurement are required)

- Calling 8000 444 0407 (expects you to run a far off indicative and give evidence of purchase)

# Chapter 4: Benefits and Pro Tips of Using iPhone 11

The 11 version iPhone had been the otherworldly replacement to iPhone XR that was greater than its antecedent, iPhone X, however, made with less expensive materials. Two new "genius" models, then again, are subsequent meet-ups to XS as well as XS Max versions, which displaced iPhone X. Though Pro and Pro Max versions of iPhone 11 are enticing cell phones with the most recent Apple technology, iPhone 11 could be said to be an amazing cellphone with its unique features. The upcoming section is about a few motivations to consider iPhone 11 rather than Apple's two new "expert" cell phones from the same series.

## 4.1 Pros of using iPhone 11

### 1. Altogether Less Expensive than iPhone 11 Pro Models

Reviews for iPhone 11 have been, to a great extent, definite with commentators applauding the new double focal point camera framework. It has a unique ultra-wide-edge focal point and Night mode, considering fresh, clear photographs even in low lighting circumstances.

Commentators likewise adulated the long battery life of iPhone 11 and the minimal effort. At $699, the gadget is considerably more reasonable than the 11 Pro and Pro Max, and besides show and camera quality, the 11 is similarly as fit as its increasingly costly partners. Analysts concur that iPhone 11 is perfect for many people because of its sticker price and list of capabilities. However, the individuals who have an iPhone XS, XS Max, or XR might not have any desire to overhaul as this is an iterative update. For those with an older version, however, iPhone 11 is an incredible phone.

After all, you can spare at any rate $300 by picking the standard iPhone 11 rather than a "Professional" 11, particularly since every one of the three new iPhones has a similar beginning stockpiling of 64 GB.

**2. Enhanced Rear, Front Cameras**

Front camera has been moved up to more megapixels. This implies you could take wide-point selfies. Furthermore, when you turn your phone to scene mode, you could capture moderate movement selfies (called Slofies).

The 11 version iPhone contains two cameras on back, a significant redesign from the specific camera that iPhone XR contains. The 11 iPhone version's cameras incorporate a sensor that is 12-megapixel wide with about multiple times quicker self-adjust in dimmer light as well as an Ultra-Wide 12-megapixel camera that catches multiple times more scenes. The standard focal point contains f/1.8 opening, whereas the ultra-wide-edge focal point contains an f/2.4 gap and a 120-degree area of view. A zooming focal point is just useful for optical zooming, which does not lose any detail contrasted with advanced zooming. Besides, it is anything but an absolute necessity to have been included. If you genuinely care about cell phone photography, you may not utilize the zoom feature in the first place.

**3. Huge Magnificent Display**

The reason iPhone 11 is not much costly is because of the presentation which is an HD IPS Despite the showcase being LCD-based, the bigger size guarantees that it, besides everything, gives a vivid encounter when gaming or viewing videos. iPhone 11 has the perfect screen size: not too enormous, however not very small. The Pro Max show is considerable, while the ordinary Pro is durable, yet conceivably somewhat little for specific individuals. OLED screens, similar to those in iPhone 11 Pro and Pro Max, produce more extravagant hues and more profound complexity, so darker objects, specifically, truly look inky and not dim.

Though the LCD screen in iPhone 11 cannot put up a similar OLED impact, the Liquid Retina show, despite everything, gives an excellent picture and precise hues. It is perhaps the best LCD in any cell phone.

**4. iPhone 11 has Greater Number of Hues than the Pro Models**

iPhone 11 Pro make come in only four hues: space dark, silver, gold, and 12 PM Green. iPhone 11, nonetheless, comes in six shades: purple, yellow, green, dark, white, and red. However, Apple evacuated blue and coral choices.

**5. iPhone 11 and 11 Pro Models have Indistinguishable Front Cameras**

The 11 and 11 Pro models of iPhone contain 12-megapixel selfie camera that bolsters 4K video up to 60 casings for every second. They additionally have the equivalent TrueDepth camera framework that takes into consideration Face ID, which can open your phone and assist you with purchases.

**6. Each of the Three New iPhones has Similar Cerebrums: Apple's A13 Bionic chip**

This deal is significant. Apple's chipset – which contains the CPU, GPU, and neural motor to make your cell phone agile and power-effective – is the equivalent over every one of the three iPhones. So you should not perceive any lesser in execution by choosing the less expensive phone.

Likewise, the A13 Bionic is powerful. Apple's A11 Bionic that controlled the iPhone X was fit for 600 billion activities for every second. The A12 Bionic inside the iPhone XS and XR could manage 5 trillion tasks for each second. The new A13 Bionic, however, is fit for 8.5 trillion jobs for each second.

### 7. Picture Mode Improvements

Apple has included pet help Portrait Mode. Additionally, another Portrait Lighting highlight known as "High Key Mono" is also included.

### 8. Night Mode Feature

Night Mode includes long introduction photographs, consequently when in dim lighting conditions. Furthermore, it makes pictures in obscurity look sharper. Including the sharpness component was necessary for the Apple since Google Pixel range of gadgets has gained notoriety for the tendency to get better photographs around evening time.

### 9. Deep Fusion Feature

Apple will, before long, be discharging an element known as Deep Fusion. Deep Fusion highlight utilizes AI to improve photographs inside low to the medium gleam. It requires nine pictures before shutter button is pressed, including four short photos and four optional pictures. What is more, when you press the screen button, it requires one prolonged exposure. Under one second, neural motor breaks down the blend of lengthy and short pictures and selects the finest among them. Furthermore, it chooses all pixels and moves from pixel to pixel (experiencing 24 millions of pixels) so as to advance for the detail plus the low commotion.

### 10. Ground-breaking Processor (detailed comparison in point 6 above)

Apple coordinated the Bionic chipset, A13 in iPhone 11. A13 has been more force productive than A12 to give 1 hour enhanced battery life contrasted with iPhone XR.

### 11. Updated Sound

iPhone 11 contains spatial sound help incorporated with the speakers. It has got Dolby Atmos' assistance. The spatial mindfulness highlight is made conceivable with Apple's recently structured U1 chip alongside the Ultra-Wideband innovation. This provides you with a strong sound-like understanding while you tune in to music, play games, and watch recordings.

### 12. IP68 Rating

11 version iPhone contains IP68 rating, a hop from iPhone XR's IP67 rating. Having IP68 rating, iPhone 11 can deal with getting 4 meters submerged into the water for about 30 minutes.

### 13. QuickTake

iPhone 11 range of gadgets is increasing a component known as QuickTake feature. QuickTake element permits you to grab the screen catch to begin recording without escaping the Photo mode.

**14. Strong Battery Life**

Just referenced before, Apple's A13 processor renders battery increasingly productive. Thus, it contains one more hour than iPhone XR. Likewise, iPhone 11 bolsters remote charging and quick charging help, although it not necessarily accompanies the 18W charger for that matter.

iPhone 11's battery backs as long as 17 hours including video playback (i.e. downloaded). Likewise, it could also incorporate 10 hours including video playback when streaming. Furthermore, with sound playback, it underpins as long as 65 hours.

Therefore, iPhone 11 and 11 Pro alike, have large batteries. The standard 11 Pro ought to have about the equivalent 16.5 to 17.5 long periods of life. However, the 11 Pro Max ought to get an incredible 18.5 to 19.5 long periods of life, as per Apple. iPhone 11 and 11 Pro models share a significant number of similar specs.

Each of the three models incorporates the equivalent:

- Dust resistance and splash rating (IP68)
- Spatial sound with Dolby Atmos support
- Wi-Fi 6, Bluetooth and LTE support
- Double SIM support

- Photograph and video highlights like Night mode, QuickTake, and Deep Fusion
- The new U1 chip for direct AirDrop record transfers

While iPhone 11 Pro has a couple of points of interest over the standard 11 – a predominant showcase, a zooming focal point, marginally higher water resistance, as well as somewhat quicker cell network – those distinctions presumably do not legitimize a $300+ value contrast for a great many people.

In case you are going back and forth between these smartphones, decide on the more moderate iPhone 11. This might be the final year of the "indent" – that shuts out a segment of your iPhone's showcase that permits space for the forward-looking camera framework – and you should update once the iPhone embraces a cleaner look. Besides, 5G support is supposed to be provided with the following year's iPhones, and you may need a bit of that activity in only a year from now.

Except if you have not updated in years and urgently need the maximum out of Apple's offer, many people will be exceptionally content with the standard iPhone 11.

This implies you can go through less cash now on a quality phone, and set aside more cash for the future when you are genuinely prepared to put resources into an all-new encounter. You can find out about Apple's new iPhones and preorder them on Apple's site. Presumably, all the latest iPhone 11 models will discharge to people in general on Friday, September 20.

As a final thought, iPhone 11 takes nearly everything that makes iPhone 11 Pro and Pro Max extraordinary and crushes it down into a bundle that is $50, not exactly a year ago's modest model. For every other person, it is the least demanding approach to experience present-day lead iPhone execution without dropping $1,000.

## 4.2 Tips for using iPhone 11 Like a Pro

As clear as they seem to be, iPhones are likewise home to different concealed tips and hacks that you probably might not know. We shall attempt to address that by featuring some slick stunts that could help you in regular daily existence.

If you have any of the past version iPhones and are running iOS 13 effectively, a considerable lot of these highlighted tips, despite everything, would apply.

So get some tea, plunk down and burrow through a portion of these tips, and genuinely get to hold with the most recent programming on your iPhone.

**1. Secure your iPhone 11**

Your iPhone 11 is significant, portable, and simple to be snatched or stolen. Therefore, you would need to put forth a valiant effort to make sure about your gadget's or data's security and safety.

Head to Settings, and in Face ID and Passcode, have Face ID be utilized to open your phone. In Display and Brightness, set Auto-Lock to 30 seconds except if your iPhone never goes out. Make sure Erase Data (swipe down to discover this choice) is on, wipe your iPhone after ten fizzled password endeavors.

Look at the new Find My application, which combines area and tracking of the gadget. You can set up area following for your iPhone, and perform activities on a lost device, including playing a sound, checking it lost, or - if all else fails - deleting it entirely.

**2. Camera and the Photos**

**Rapidly Catch Video:** One fresh interface in camera application is the capacity to record a video inside Photo mode quickly.

You should simply drag the screen catch towards camera switcher, which would consequently change to the video and begin recording when you release.

**A fast Explosion of Photographs:** In a comparative move to snappy video catch, you could drag shutter towards camera move to rapidly snatch an eruption of pictures.

**Switch between Zoom, Wide and Ultra-Wide:** To rapidly shift between the few cameras at the backside of iPhone, simply click the little "1x" symbol onto the screen. Provided that you would preferably zoom all the more easily, you can simply swipe down or up your screen and observe as zoom scroll-wheel advances.

**Take Slofies:** Smartphones have had the option to take moderate movement recordings for quite a while; however, with iPhone 11, the Apple has empowered it from forward-looking camera. To make a purported Slofie, change to Slow Mo choice inside the camera application and simply tap camera switcher symbol to adjust to front camera. Then press record. That way, you will have a moderate movement selfie video.

**Quickly Access the Settings:** While you shoot a photograph, you should rapidly access your settings flips. You should simply swipe up over the shutter catch.

You will get a column of choices remembering exchanging the glimmer for, changing the perspective proportion, empowering live photographs, setting a clock, or picking a live channel.

**Shoot Night Photograph:** This one is simple. When it is dull enough, the phone naturally identifies it and offers night custom shot as alternative. A little symbol would be created that would look somewhat like a smaller than usual Death Star. (Then again, maybe a concealed moon, in case you need to be exhausting). Click on it, then you would shoot a night photograph.

**Expand Night Mode Presentation:** Having the night mode empowered by default, the iPhone consequently sets the introduction time (for the most part about 3 seconds). In case you need to expand it, you could simply broaden it by hauling down the clock interface close to the shade button.

**Sweep a QR code:** Scroll down to uncover the Control Center screen, then tap small QR code symbol. At that point, you will get custom QR filtering UI that utilizes camera and contains a torch symbol to turn the glimmer on.

**Enable or Impair Smart HDR:** Among the latest iPhone's camera headways includes Smart HDR, that helps support hues, light, as well as detail in troublesome lighting conditions. In case there is a need to turn it on and off physically, you can make a beeline for Settings, then the Camera and locate Smart HDR flip switch.

**Lighting Effects for Portrait:** To take Portrait Mode snaps with feigned lighting impacts, first visit shoot in the Portrait mode. This could be done in two ways; by long-squeezing the camera symbol and picking the Portrait alternate way, or opening camera application and choosing the Portrait choice in there. Presently you can simply press and retain the base of the casing where it is mentioned "Natural Lighting", then look through the alternatives.

**Lightning Impact Brightness Alterations:** With latest iPhones, you could alter the quality of lightning impact in the wake of taking Portrait shot. Move to Photos, then choose the photograph you need to change; at that point, select "alter." You would find slider at base of screen. Swipe the right end to build more brightness, or swipe left corner to diminish it.

**Empower Video Recording, 60fps 4K:** Move to Settings, then Camera, then select Record Video, afterward pick 60fps 4K choice to take shots at the loftiest goal and casing rate conceivable on iPhone.

**Capture 1080p Moderate Movement at 240fps:** Like the previous one, move to Settings, then Camera, afterwards select "Record Slow-mo". Then pick the most outstanding speed choice.

**Take Live Photo:** Go to the camera enabling Photo mode, after which tap the symbol that resembles three rings, (the external ring would be dabbed). On the off chance that it is yellow, then Live Photos has been enabled.

**Keep the Actual Photograph while Utilizing Live Photo Impacts:** Once you pick among many Live Photo impacts, it stores it on the phone in the form of a video, instead of a photograph. If you need to retain the first shot as still photograph also, simply select the share symbol and press "duplicate", then spare another duplicate of the first photograph. (You will have to do so before changing Live Photo impact - or simply return to the first Live Photo format and perform it at that point). You could apply filters as well, to your live photograph.

**Instructions to Integrate People in the Photos Application:** Photographs in iOS can filter your photographs and identify individuals and spots. In case you discover that the application has selected a similar individual, yet claims they are various individuals, you can combine the collections. To perform this, you would need to visit the Photos application > Albums and then select People and the Places. You would need to tap on "Select", located at the upper right of screen and afterward select the pictures of the individuals you need to combine, at that point, tap "Merge".

**Effective Method to Alter Style of the Memories Film:** You could either choose the default film mode from the Apple, or could alter it to fix a bunch of various styles. Move towards Memory you need to alter, tap on "play" symbol on the fundamental picture, and at that point, tap again on video when it is playing. You will currently observe slideshow style alternatives like Sentimental, Dreamy, Chill, Gentle, and Delighted, among many. You could likewise pick between Medium, Short or the Long options.

**Search Photo Collections:** Visit the Photos application and push on the amplifying glass. Prompt recommendations incorporate narrowing your picture outcomes by "One Year Ago", "Nearby", as well as "Favorites". You can also type in loads of various inquiries such as, months or spot names. Or a mix of both.

**Approach Siri to Bring a Photograph for You:** The Siri feature would now be able to look for your photographs dependent on their data and standards. Request her to locate a particular photograph from July 14, 2015, for example, and it will do only that. Amazing right?

**Upload the Photo Bursts:** Move to Settings; at that point, select your name located at the head of screen. At that point, move to "iCloud", then "Photos", and then "Upload the Burst Photos" option. Doing so would back up all photographs in burst instead of merely the most loved one.

**Most Loved Photographs:** If you have photographs that you need to stamp so that they could be displayed to others rapidly later, as opposed to scanning or looking for them, the photos could be added to favorites. To render this, just discover the picture you need to mark favorite and then hit the heart symbol. To locate them immediately when you move to Photos application, push on Albums symbol at the base right, at that point select the Favorites collection.

**Know Where You Snapped a Picture:** In Albums segment of the application, tap on "People and Places" area and pick the "Places" collection. You would find the entirety of the areas you have taken photographs in, also which shots were captured in which areas of world. Zooming provides increasingly specific areas whereas tapping "Grid" records the regions within the specific view.

**AE/AF Lock:** To alter the presentation or the focal point of the shot, press anyplace on screen, then it would change immediately. To bolt that focus or exposure, press and hang on screen till the given square box secures through the "lock-in".

**3. Control Center Hacks**

**Include New Controls:** Like the past adaptation of iOS, you can include and expel controls from Control Center. Head to Settings > Control Center > Customize Controls and pick which controls you would prefer to add.

**Enact Screen Recording:** One of the choices included in 2018, which you can add to the Control Center, is Screen Recording. Ensure that you include the control, open Control Center, and press the symbol that resembles a strong white hover inside a slight white ring.

Beginning now and into the foreseeable future, it will record everything that occurs on your screen. Press the control again when you are finished, and it will store a video to your Photos application consequently.

**Reorganizing Controls:** If you want to alter the request for those controls you have included, press and hold three-bar symbol on the privilege of the control that you would prefer to move; at that point, move it here and there the rundown to any place you would prefer that to be.

**Extend Controls:** Certain controls could turn out to be full screen, simply long push on control that you need to grow, and the control would cover the screen.

**Turn your Own Hotspot On:** The availability control just has four alternatives in it, by default. Once you long-press to extend it, you will have full-screen control along with two additional choices. You would need to select the individual hotspot symbol to turn it on.

**Rapidly Switch Where Sound is Played:** An amazing element is the capacity to alter where music or audio is playing. When the music is being played, through the Spotify, Apple Music, or any other place, long push on music control. You could also tap little symbol in top end of music control.

That would raise a spring, demonstrating accessible gadgets that could be played through. It could be associated with the Bluetooth speaker, headphones, iPhone, Apple TV, or any other AirPlay gadget.

**Set a Brisk Clock:** Instead of making a beeline for the clock application, you could long push on the clock symbol, at that point, move up and down on full-screen to turn a clock somewhere in the range of one moment to two complete hours in length.

**Get to HomeKit Gadgets:** Open the Control Center, then afterward click on little symbol that resembles a house.

**4. iCloud Tips**

**Discover your Gadgets (and Companions):** Find my Friends has gone, yet that does not mean you cannot discover them any longer. Apple simply moved all the areas following administrations into one "Find My" application. Simply open it up, and you will see a tab for contacts and another for gadgets. It is straightforward.

**Turn on your iCloud Drive:** Move to Settings, tap on your name/ID at the top, and move to iCloud > iCloud Drive. Switch it on or off.

**Deal with your Storage:** Move to Settings, at that point, your name/ID > iCloud > Manage Storage. From here, you can perceive how much stockpiling you have, the amount you have left, and decide to purchase additional.

**Family Sharing:** Instead of having your iTunes account on the entirety of your family's iPhones and iPads, you would now be able to set up Family Sharing for up to 5 individuals. Visit Settings; at that point, tap your name/ID at the top and pick the "Family Sharing" choice.

**Secure iCloud Keychain Access:** Move to Settings, at that point, your name/ID at the top > iCloud > Keychain, and switch it on or off.

**Access iCloud Drive Documents:** iOS 11 presented Files application in 2017. Look for it; at that point, click the "Browse" tab, and you will see the entirety of the documents and organizers in your record.

**5. Display and Home Screen**

**Expel Stock Applications:** Since the iOS 11 update in 2017, Apple has permitted you to evacuate the default Apple applications like Compass, Stocks, and others. To do so, essentially tap and hang on the application symbol for some time until it begins squirming and afterward tap the "x".

You will be approached to affirm your choice. To get them back, just quest for the application being referred to in the App Store.

**Allow Dark Mode:** Move to Settings > Display and Brightness and now flip on the Dark Mode switch. You can likewise get it to change dependent on schedule or dawn/dusk consequently.

**Modify Home Screen Symbols:** Now that there is no more weight delicate showcase, a portion of the long press and power contact activities have changed. There are two different ways to modify your application symbols. Either long push on an application and tap "rearrange applications" in the spring up menu, or simply long-press and drag the logo before the spring up menu has even shown up.

**Darken Wallpapers with Dark Mode:** A significant piece of iOS 13's update is the new dark mode choice. With a couple of the reinstalled backdrops, you can get the picture obscure and change at whatever point dark mode is empowered. Explore Settings > Wallpaper and make sure that the "dark appearance dims wallpaper" flip is turned on.

At that point, hit "choose new wallpaper" and pick one from "Stills" or "Live," which has the little overshadowing symbol in the base right corner.

Presently, at whatever point dim mode is empowered, the backdrop will likewise go dim.

**Zoomed or Standard Display:** Since iPhone 6 Plus, you have got the option to pick between two goal options. You can change the presentation setting from Standard or Zoomed. To switch between the two - if you have adjusted your perspective after arrangement - move to Settings > Display and Brightness > Display Zoom and select Standard or Zoomed.

**Rapidly Add Numerous Applications to an Envelope:** This one has been around for a few years, yet rather than just exclusively, gradually hauling each application in turn into an organizer, you can pack them together rapidly. Long-press an app and drag it on the head of another symbol; at that point, fast tap some other applications to frame a skimming gathering of applications.

**Allow Display for True Tone:** To get the iPhone's screen to naturally alter its shading parity and temperature to coordinate the surrounding light in the room, head to Control Center, and long-press the screen splendor slider. Presently tap the True Tone button. You can likewise visit the Settings > Display and Brightness and flip the "Genuine Tone" switch.

**Night Shift:** As well as True Tone, there is an alternative Night Shift that removes blue light helping your eyes unwind. Raise Control Center, at that point, long-press the presentation splendor slider and select the Night Shift button.

**Enable Apple Pay:** Again, the "Sleep/Wake" button is the key here. Double-tap it, and it will raise your Apple Wallet; at that point, examine your face, and it will request that you hold your phone near the installment machine.

**6. Console Tips**

**Go Single-Handed:** QuickType console of iOS 13 permits you to type single-handed, extraordinary on the greater gadgets like XS Max make of iPhone. Press and grab the globe symbol and pick either left or the right-sided console. It contracts the console and shifts it aside from the presentation. Return to full measure by clicking the little bolt.

**Utilize your Console as Trackpad:** As the 3D Touch is formally gone, you can no longer utilize the trackpad highlight by squeezing hard on the console. Rather, presently you have to long-push on the space bar, and it will enable a similar action; presently, swipe around the keypad to move the cursor around.

**Strike to Type:** One of the new iOS 13 highlights is the capacity to type on the console by simply swiping over the letters. Start on the first letter of the word, and simply swipe through the others to type rapidly. At the point when you need a twofold letter in the word, simply hold that letter for a brief timeframe before proceeding through the swiping movement.

**Include Third-Party Consoles:** Install the application (SwiftKey or Gboard are genuine models) and adhere to the application's guidelines. Sooner or later, it will request that you visit Settings > General > Keyboard > Keyboards and include the outsider console.

**Shortcuts for Text Substitution:** As in every single earlier year, one of iOS' most helpful console arrangements is making short-codes that transform into full words or expressions. Explore Settings > General > Keyboard > Text Replacement. We think that it is helpful to have one for a location that fills in naturally at whatever point we incorrectly spell "address," including an extra "s" toward the end.

### 7. Restrictions and Notifications

**Convey Notifications Unobtrusively:** One intriguing new tool for the notifications' management lets you send notices from explicit applications to Notification Center without alarming you with a sound, application identification, or illuminating your lock screen. In case you need to utilize this component, swipe left on a notification (or gathering of notices from a particular application) and choose the "manage" option. Then click "Deliver Quietly".

**Extend the Notifications Clusters:** iOS 13 groups numerous notifications from the equivalent application in a little virtual heap on your lock screen, by default. To grow them and see the entirety of the individual notices in a rundown, simply tap on the heap.

**Set Application Limits:** In the "Screentime" menu, "App Limits" comes next. Pick this

choice and select "Add Limit" while picking which class of applications you need to add a period breaking point. Select the category and afterward, "Add" before picking a period breaking point and hitting "Set".

**Restrict Content Access:** As a feature of the substance/security limitations, pick the "Content restrictions" choice, and here you can confine improper content access involving sites, TV shows, books, sound, and much more.

**Pick "Always Allowed" Applications:** By default, iOS 13 sorts out applications into different classes, both advantageous and poorly designed. For example, WhatsApp and Facebook Messenger are generalized with the likes of person to person communication applications. So on the off chance that they are your essential correspondence applications, you will need to ensure there is no restriction.

In the primary Screentime settings menu, click "Always Allowed" and select the applications you need to guarantee are not affected when you set the time limits.

**Content and Privacy Limitations:** This segment is also inside the principle Screentime settings menu and especially fruitful if you are a parent with children who use iOS gadgets. Utilizing it, you can confine all kinds of options and content, incorporating in-application buys and iTunes, area administrations, publicizing, etc. It is worth it.

## 8. Notes Tips

**Turning on Passwords in Notes:** To secure individual notes using passwords, switch to Settings > Notes > Password. Here you can set a default secret key for every one of your notes, and you can empower Face ID as well.

**Collaborate and Share on Notes:** There is another offer symbol inside Notes that resembles an individual's outline and a "+" symbol near it. Click on it, and you could include contacts who could view and make amendments progressively.

**Lock the Note:** You would need to open Notes, at that point, long push on the required notes in the dropdown. Press "Lock Note" appearing in the pop-down menu. Then type your secret password, and it will be bolted. You can likewise render that by opening the note, squeezing the offer symbol, and afterward, "Lock Note" symbol. That only add lock symbol to Note. Then click on the symbol to bolt the Note. Subsequently, when you get to it, you would require password. Be cautioned on the off chance that you are attempting to get to it on an iOS gadget you have not refreshed to 9.3 and subsequent version; you would not have an option to get to it on the gadget in question.

**Notes (handwritten):** Open Notes application; at that point, tap new note symbol in the base right, then get the pen device over the console. Then write away until you are done.

**Store Attachments in the Notes:** There is additional help for Notes through System-Wide Share option. In this way, while inside Safari, for example, tap on the Share catch to spare connections, like the connection or record, to another or the existing Note. Likewise, in Notes feature, there is an Attachment program that sorts out connections in single view (press the grid symbol located in lower-left end).

**9. Maps Tips**

**Set Favored Vehicle Type in Apple Maps:** If you discover you possibly ever use Apple Maps when strolling, you can set the favored vehicle type. To transform it between Walking, Driving, and Public Transport, click Settings > Maps and pick the one you need.

**3D Structures in Maps:** New 3D structures have been included by the Apple inside the Street View elective in iOS 13 Maps. However, it is constrained to explicit urban areas. Move towards San Francisco inside Maps application and click the latest optics symbol in the application to enable the Street View.

**Use ARKit with FlyOver:** Couple of years back, Apple built up its personal Maps application, complete with Flyover, virtual 3D renditions of significant urban communities. Presently you can check out 3D urban communities simply by making a shift in your iPhone. Quest for a substantial city - such as London or the New York - at that point choose the "FlyOver" alternative. At that point, you should simply move your gadget and check out the city.

**Utilize Indoor Guides:** For the initial run through inside Apple Maps application, iOS 11 empowered indoor planning to discover the essential shopping centers. It has gradually been developed from that point forward, and you could attempt it in an entire host of mainstream global air terminals. To utilize indoor guides, simply look for an upheld area and squeeze-to-zoom in till the open air regions go dull dark. That way, you could peek inside the premises.

**Move along the Building Levels through Indoor Guides:** When you are into the building map, you will find a number on right corner of screen. Press it, and afterward, pick a story level.

**10. Safari Tips**

**Stop Sites Following You:** Visit Settings > Safari and afterward flip the "Prevent cross-site tracking" option on.

**Access Stored Passwords:** Thanks to iCloud, Safari can store your secret word over the entirety of your gadgets. Move to Settings > Passwords, and Accounts > Website and App Passwords, at that point, sign in utilizing your Face ID scanner. Here you could find all of the passwords which have been saved and oversee them.

**Figuring out the Text in Safari:** To Discover text in a Safari page, select the "Share" option on a page to see a "Find on Page" choice (it surfaces drop-up over the console).

# Conclusion

The iPhone 11 is another iPhone that is progressively reasonable and still packs in massive amount of highlights that make it an enticing overhaul from a more established iPhone or Android phone. There are numerous things the iPhone 11 can do. Inside this guide, there are the most energizing things you can do with the iPhone 11. Regardless of whether you are hoping to realize precisely what your new iPhone 11 can do or are contemplating purchasing the new iPhone, this is the complete guide of cool things the iPhone 11 can do. You do not have to purchase a massive amount of frill or another case to utilize these highlights. After you find out about these cool things, you can figure out how to use the iPhone 11 to shed pounds, get fit as a fiddle, set aside cash, and even bring in money. As you become familiar with the iPhone 11, you can utilize this manual for discovering the amount of iPhone 11 stockpiling you need and data about which iPhone 11 shade to purchase.

The guide book would further enable its readers to know how exactly to get their iPhone 11 ensured if the phone gets stolen, damaged, or otherwise lost.

Readers would be exposed to the policies adopted by AppleCare+ in case of planned and unplanned harm to the device. iPhone 11 users would learn more about the operating system of iPhone 11, i.e., iOS 13, along with some prominent updations therein. Siri application, Find My app, Health app, and iCloud Drive are all available in the previous versions of the iPhone. The said applications have however been, enormously update for good in the latest iPhone 11 versions. This ultimate guide would let the keen users know that with all such updations and a unique in-league price, why iPhone 11 is such an ideal buy. If used adequately, the users' iPhone 11 journey would be an unforgettable one! We wish them the best of their iPhone11 learning experience.

Printed in Dunstable, United Kingdom

67334541R00080